Room to Move

Nelson

Other books by Peter Forrestal and Jo-Anne Reid:

Space to Dream (English Workshop Two)
Time to Tell (English Workshop Three)

Room to Move

ENGLISH WORKSHOP ONE

Peter Forrestal and Jo-Anne Reid

adapted by Averil Brooker

Nelson

Thomas Nelson and Sons Ltd
Nelson House   Mayfield Road
Walton-on-Thames   Surrey
KT12 5PL   UK

51 York Place
Edinburgh
EH1 3JD   UK

Thomas Nelson (Hong Kong) Ltd
Toppan Building 10/F
22A Westlands Road
Quarry Bay   Hong Kong

First published by Thomas Nelson Australia, 480 La Trobe Street,
Melbourne, Victoria 3000, 1983 (under ISBN 0–17–006198–1)

This edition published by Thomas Nelson & Sons Ltd, 1987
ISBN 0–17–432 1732
NPN:01

Cover by Keith McEwan
Illustrated by Tom Kurema, Jo-Anne Reid and Peter Joyce
Typeset in Century Schoolbook and Helvetica
by ProComp Productions Pty Ltd, Adelaide
Printed in Hong Kong

Contents

To the teacher

Room to Move is a book about language use. It is designed to enable students to develop their ability to use language by exploring their own world and the world of literature. It gives them the opportunity to use their language, and the language of literature, for a variety of purposes and audiences – all of which are designed to be 'real' for the student.

Because we believe that a clear learning sequence is necessary for students to move from information to understanding, *Room to Move* is very much concerned with classroom management. With most activities, we suggest a learning sequence which takes students from the stage where they acquire information, through an exploration of that information into situations where they use the information or look at it in a variety of ways. Students are generally required to present what they have learned to an audience and then to reflect on the outcome.

Writing activities have been designed so that students will see the importance of drafting, revising and editing in the writing process.

Students are given a wide range of opportunities for self-expression; to clarify their ideas and sort out their misunderstandings in the early stages of the learning process, to move from tentative exploration to clear and articulate communication of what they have learned in the later stages.

Room to Move is intended as a core textbook for the English course in the first year of secondary school. It obviously needs to be supplemented by a wide range of other resources; fiction from the school library, anthologies of short stories, poetry and drama scripts. Many teachers will also wish to study some aspects of the media – especially film, television, radio and newspapers – as part of the English course.

We have indicated some occasions when the study of language can arise naturally from the work in which students are engaged. In our opinion, students should be given help with grammar, punctuation and spelling, either individually or in small groups, where their writing indicates the need for such assistance.

We see literature as central to any English course. Students' need to develop an awareness of and sensitivity towards literature. Reading, writing, talking, listening and thinking about literature and their own experiences helps them to understand these more clearly and helps in the development of their functional literacy.

Because of the importance of collaborative learning and the value of talk in the learning process, the handling of group work plays a central part in classroom management.

All the activities presented to students in *Room to Move* are designed for the classroom organised into small friendship groups of two, three or four students.

The book is designed to encourage students to develop their own particular interests and skills, while catering at the same time for differing needs and abilities.

Obviously there will be many occasions when students will ask for help from the teacher. This symbol means that teacher action or assistance has been specifically mentioned.

Peter Forrestal and Jo-Anne Reid

Scope and sequence chart

	FOCUS	READING	WRITING	TALKING	LITERARY AND LANGUAGE CONCEPTS
Ch. 1	Introduction to: • other students • small group work • talking and writing tasks	Poetry by Spike Milligan and Michael Rosen	• Personal experience • Items for class newspaper	• Introductions • Interview • Panel discussion • Telling a story	• Dictionary • Filling in forms • Comparative and superlative • Importance of your own personal experience in producing literature
Ch. 2	Introducing the journal	Student opinions and comments on journal writing	Student choice Journal writing	Full class discussion about using the journal	Importance of expressive writing in the development of students' writing ability
Ch. 3	Drafting and editing and the writing process	• Students drafting and editing their own writing • Examples of student writing			• Understanding the writing process • Importance of drafting and editing in writing
Ch. 4	Writing for a particular audience	• Short story: 'Nothing to be Afraid Of'	• Autobiographical incident • Book (writing a child's story) • Letter • Notes for story	• Small group talk about short story (introduction to exploratory talk) • Chat with primary school child	• Plot and theme • Third person narration
Ch. 5	Suspense	• Short story: 'Spit Nolan' • Poem: 'The Highwayman'	• Writing the story of the 'Highwayman' from another point of view • Own story using suspense	• Drama based on a poem • Exchanging information about suspense with other groups	• Suspense • Metaphors • Point of view
Ch. 6	Ballads	Wide selection of traditional ballads	• Notes about ballads • Writing a ballad	• Read ballads aloud • Making up introduction to ballad • Improvisation • Sharing information with students from other groups • Choral speaking	• Australian, British and American traditional ballads • Characteristics of a ballad
Ch. 7	Folk tales	Folk tales: 'Tattercoats', 'Cap O' Rushes' and 'Rushen Coatie'	• Written argument • Write argument in pairs • Play • Ballad	• Interview • Group discussion	• Comparing stories in terms of plot, characters, dialogue, setting and their ending • Argument
Ch. 8	Close examination of a theme	• Short story: 'The Flying Machine' • Essay: 'It's the Letrit' • Song: 'Where do the children play?'	• Writing an argument • Writing poetry • Presenting a written survey	• Group discussion of a theme • Whole class discussion • Arguing in pairs • Debating	• Examination of a theme through literature • Comparing a film with a short story

A Place for Me

Like an eagle, on the edge of the wind,
Like a wild horse that leads the herd,
I search for room
A gap I can fill
A place in the sky.
      Anywhere?
         Everywhere!
     Room to move.

Elizabeth

1 Introductions

Hello . . . how are you?
Hello . . . who are you?
Hello . . . are you . . . ?
Hello . . . ah . . . ?

Look around the classroom. How many people do you **really** know?

Just as important, how many people **really** know you?

This is an introductory unit of work:

- it introduces you to the way you'll be working when you use this book in class (mainly in small groups)

- it helps you to start the year by introducing yourself to somebody else, learning to introduce people to each other, and learning how to be introduced to other people.

INTRODUCTION: what does it mean?

The word 'introduction' came into English from the Latin word **introducere** which was made up of **intro** = into, and **ducere** = lead or bring, so **introduction** means to lead into, or to bring into.

This chapter uses introduction in both senses of the word:

- to lead you into the rest of the book, and

- to bring you into your place as an important member of your class.

Application for a British Visitor's Passport

Photograph	Stamp of issuing office	For Passport Office use only	Passport number

Documents produced by
Holder   Spouse   Children

Height measurement

Height in passports is shown in metric units. A conversion table follows: ft = feet, ins = inches, m = metres

ft	ins	m	ft	ins	m
4	0	1.22	5	3	1.60
4	1	1.24	5	4	1.63
4	2	1.27	5	5	1.65
4	3	1.30	5	6	1.68
4	4	1.32	5	7	1.70
4	5	1.35	5	8	1.73
4	6	1.37	5	9	1.75
4	7	1.40	5	10	1.78
4	8	1.42	5	11	1.80
4	9	1.45	6	0	1.83
4	10	1.47	6	1	1.85
4	11	1.50	6	2	1.88
5	0	1.52	6	3	1.90
5	1	1.55	6	4	1.93
5	2	1.57	6	5	1.96

Please write in ink using CAPITAL LETTERS. Tick yes or no boxes as appropriate.

1 Passport holder

Mr, Mrs, Miss, Ms or title:

Surname

Forename(s) or Christian name(s)

Maiden surname (if any)

Date of birth   Age

Town of birth

Country of birth

Present address in the UK and Islands

Post code   Your height in metres

Visible distinguishing marks

2 Particulars of wife/husband if to be included in passport. See Notes overleaf

Surname

Forename(s) or Christian name(s)

Maiden surname (if any)

Date of birth

Town of birth

Country of birth

Height in metres

Visible distinguishing marks

3 Children under 16 years of age if to be included in passport. See Note overleaf

Christian names or forenames	Surname	Town and country of birth	Date of birth	Relationship to you (eg son or daughter)

4 Parent's or guardian's consent for a person under 18 years old and for included children

Not needed if the person is married or in HM Forces.

If the person is illegitimate, the mother must give consent (but see below).

If a court order exists, the person awarded custody of the child/children must sign.

I (full name)

address

being the (relationship to child/children eg father, mother)

consent to the issue of passport facilities to him/her/them.

I confirm that my rights over the child/children have not been altered by a court order.

Signature

5 Declaration

To be filled in by all applicants

If the passport is for a child under 16, a parent must fill in and sign this section.

Do you/does the child already have a passport?

yes ☐   no ☐

If your wife/husband is to be included in the passport, does she/he already have a passport?

yes ☐   no ☐

If you have/the child has a passport already, give it to the Passport Office with this application.

See Note overleaf

If you cannot give the passport to the Passport Office: please state why (eg lost, stolen or unavailable)

Date of loss or theft

Have you reported this to the police?   yes ☐   no ☐

If yes please state where and when

Number of lost/stolen passport (if known)

Place of issue

Date of issue

Signature of applicant

Date

If the passport is found by me or returned to me, I undertake to send it to the Passport Office, Belfast or, if I am abroad, to the nearest British Consulate or High Commission.

I, the applicant (I, the wife/husband of the applicant) declare that:

I have read and understood the Notes overleaf

I, and those to be included in the passport are British citizens, British Dependent Territories citizens or British Overseas citizens

no other passport application is being made for me/us

none of us - if previously returned to the United Kingdom at HM Government expense - still owes the cost of the repatriation

the information given is to the best of my knowledge correct

I am today in the United Kingdom

I know that it is a criminal offence knowingly to make a false statement in this application

Signature of wife/husband if to be included in passport

Date

Introducing each other

Filling in forms

Have you ever filled in a form that asks you questions about yourself? You might like to try filling in the Passport Application on the opposite page.

Filling in forms can be difficult. You'll need to read this form carefully before you fill it in. Your teacher might make some copies of the form for you to use. Some sections on the form will not apply to you and some are for **official use only** so remember to leave these blank.

Forms like this one give the reader just a skeleton outline of information about you. They do not say at all what sort of person you are. So, to make it more interesting, try some **individual** writing.

Make notes about yourself so that another person from your group can use them to introduce you to someone else. You might like to use the information from the form, and then think of some other points:

- your likes and dislikes,
- your thoughts about school this year,
- your hopes for the future,
- things you're really good at doing,
- your successes in the past,
- any other important things about you.

Pairs work

In pairs, introduce yourselves to each other, and then explain your notes to your partner. Together you have to prepare your introductions to the rest of the group. Help one another with the introductions and when you are both ready, have a practice.

Group work

In your group of four, take turns to introduce your partner. Each person speaks only once. Use the notes you made in pairs to help.

You'll need to listen carefully to the introductions, because each person will now move on to introduce a **different** group member to two new people from another group. You can take notes to help you, if you need to.

To form your **new groups**, one person from each pair stays in the same place, while the other two people move **together** to a different group.

The first two people introduce each other to the two new people, and then the two new people make their introductions.

If you want to find out more about the two new people you have just met, spend a few minutes asking questions about anything mentioned in the introductions that interests you.

Reflection

Now move back to your own group, and tell each other about the new people you have just met.

● Think about how you introduced your partner.

● Find out from him or her how well you made the introduction.

● What did you learn from this activity?

● Do you think introductions are important? Why?

Telling tales

This is a writing session that will help you to get to know the deepest secrets of your classmates. Everyone, including your teacher, writes down **the most embarrassing experience*** they can remember.

Be honest. Spend a few minutes thinking about your most embarrassing experience, then jot down a few words or phrases that will help you to put the story in order. Try to write your story so that the whole class will clearly understand why it was so embarrassing. You will be writing your story **anonymously** but you might find it helpful to let someone you trust have a look before you finish to make sure that your story is clear.

When everyone has finished, put the stories in a box, so that they can then be read out for the whole class to enjoy.

Decide which of the embarrassing experiences you heard about is, in your private opinion, the **most** embarrassing. You could talk about this with the other members of your group to see what they thought.

* You may prefer to try other topics instead. Some suggestions:
My most frightening day,
My happiest experience,
A most eventful day . . .

The first class newspaper

The Class Newspaper can be produced throughout the year, and the contents will change according to the work you're doing. The first Class Newspaper should be aimed at finding out more about each other, and so you need to have **all** class members contributing. Here's a way to go about it:

1. **Decide** what you want to contribute:

- an exciting day in your life,
- what you like to do after school,
- the day you got into trouble,
- a scary experience you've had,

● an important person in your life,

● your thoughts on school,

● anything else that tells others more about you.

2. **Think** about it:
Make some notes to remind you of the most important points you have thought of.

3. **Tell** your story or explain your thoughts to your group, using the notes you made, and write down any suggestions or questions they have.

4. **Write** your first draft of the contribution you will make to the Class Newspaper. Use the notes and comments from your group if they are helpful.

5. Pass your first draft around the group for one or two of them to read, correct any mistakes you have made, or improve anything that they think doesn't sound quite right.

6. When all the corrections have been made, decide on how your group is going to present its contribution. Each group will be responsible for one page of the Class Newspaper. Look at some real newspapers for ideas on size and **layout**. Once the whole class has decided on the size of the pages, the group needs to decide on the amount of space for each of the articles. Your teacher will provide you with sheets of backing paper cut to the size of the pages.

7. Ask your teacher to write the Editorial for this first issue.

8. When you know exactly how your group's page is going to look, make the final copy of your article to suit. Paste the final copies onto the sheets of backing paper.

9. As your group's sheet is finished, display it on the notice board, or on a wall, until everybody has had a chance to read all the pages.

10. After display, staple all the sheets together for future reading. You might like to present your paper to the school library so that other classes can read it, or you might choose to keep it in your own classroom.

Oral work

By now you should be finding out quite a bit about your class-mates, and you should be getting to know your own group very well . . . For this activity, the class will need to divide into new groups of up to four people – each group made up of people who occupy the same position in their families:

> **Elder or eldest**
> **Middle or one of the middle children**
> **Younger or youngest**
> **Only child**

If there's only one person in any of these family positions, he or she can choose another group to work with. The group would have to look at this position as well.

Make sure that you know the difference between 'elder' and 'eldest', 'younger' and 'youngest'. This information will help you to use the correct word in your own writing. Try these:

Which is the correct word – **good, better** or **best**
(a) when you are comparing two football teams who are playing a match?
(b) when you are comparing one team with all the others in the competition?

I AM GOOD

I AM BETTER THAN HER.

I AM THE BEST IN THE WHOLE CLASS.

Small group work

**What are the advantages and disadvantages
of your position in the family?**

In this activity your group will be working towards an oral
presentation either in the form of an **interview** or as part of a
panel discussion.

I'm the youngest in our house
so it goes like this:

My brother comes in and says:
'Tell him to clear the fluff
out from under his bed.'
Mum says,
'Clear the fluff
out from under your bed.'
Father says,
'You heard what your mother said.'
'What?' I say.
'The fluff,' he says.
'Clear the fluff
out from under your bed.'
So I say,
'There's fluff under his bed, too,
you know.'
So father says,
'But we're talking about the fluff
under *your* bed.'
'You will clear it up
won't you?' mum says.
So now my brother – all puffed up –
says,
'Clear the fluff
out from under your bed,
clear the fluff
out from under your bed.'
Now I'm angry. I am angry.
So I say – what shall I say?
I say,
'Shuttup Stinks
YOU CAN'T RULE MY LIFE.'

Michael Rosen

My sister Laura

My sister Laura's bigger than me
And lifts me up quite easily.
I can't lift her, I've tried and tried:
She must have something heavy inside.

Spike Milligan

Preparation

In your group discuss the advantages and then the disadvantages of occupying your position in the family. Give an example of each advantage or disadvantage to show what you mean.

Take some notes during the discussion so that you can make a group list of the advantages and disadvantages, and the examples to go with each.

This will help you to make up a **protest poster** to show your feelings about the disadvantages of being in your group's position.

Look for a catchy slogan and an eye-catching illustration for your poster.

Use your poster for the panel discussion.

Then choose one member of your group to be the interviewer, one to be the interviewee, (person who is interviewed) and one to represent your group on the panel discussion.

Whole class work
Interviews

INTERVIEWER

INTERVIEWER'S QUESTIONS

- What position would you most like to be in your family?

- How do you think your life might be different if you had been born in a different position?

- What's the worst thing about being in your position?

- What's the best thing about it?

- Help your group's interviewee work out some good answers to these questions.

- Remember that the interviewer must introduce both himself or herself, and the interviewee, before the interview begins.

Panel discussion

- One person from each group should be on the panel, and one classmember should act as Chairperson for the discussion. The Chairperson must introduce all panel members to the class, and must put prepared questions to the panel, as well as calling for questions from the audience.

- In your group, prepare one question to ask **each** of the panel members from the other groups, and give these to the Chairperson before the discussion begins.

- Remember that any other questions you want to ask the panel must be directed through the Chairperson.

Individual work – an incident from your childhood

Preparation

Talk with the other members of your group about some of the incidents in your own childhood that you remember clearly. As a group choose either of the following methods for presenting your favourite incident or adventure to the whole class.

1. *Telling a story*

Telling a story really well requires a great deal of effort, especially when you have to interest an audience of thirty or so of your classmates, and your teacher.

- Make notes of the main points of your story;

- Make sure you have an opening that will catch the audience's interest and a punchline or some other memorable ending;

- Practise telling your story – to yourself and then to your group;

- Remember there's a difference between making a speech and telling a story. When you're telling a story you should appear as relaxed and natural as possible. You'll need to be able to tell the story without any notes.

2. *Writing a story*

Choose an incident in your own childhood that you feel will make the most interesting story. Write the story in the first person – that is, using 'I'. Do not mention your own name. When your stories are ready to read, swap them around within your group and then read them to the whole class. Ask your classmates to guess who the author is.

Reflection

This chapter has tried to help you get to know your classmates, and to help you get to know the way you'll be working when you use this book in class.

Spend some time now thinking and writing for yourself, about this introductory chapter. You might like to consider these questions:

- What have you learnt?

What about working in small groups: did you enjoy working in this way?

How much did your group work as a team?

What else would you like to know about introductions, introducing people to each other, or introducing yourself to other people?

Look at your responses to the last question. Can you think of ways you could learn about these things?

Think about other people outside school, for instance, your parents or other relatives.

How do you introduce them to your friends?

How would they like to be introduced?

Perhaps you can find out.

Reading

You might enjoy some of these stories which are concerned with incidents in young people's lives.

Stories from *The Goalkeeper's Revenge and Other Stories* by Bill Naughton

N. Baldwin, *Carrie's War*

Susan Cooper, *Over Sea, Under Stone*

Alan Garner, *The Stone Book Quartet*

Jean George, *My Side of the Mountain*

Esther Hautzing, *The Endless Steppe*

Erich Kästner, *Emil and the Detectives*

C. Day Lewis, *The Otterbury Incident*

E. Nesbit, *The Railway Children*

Ivan Southall, *Hills End*

Armstrong Sperry, *The Boy Who Was Afraid*

Mildred Taylor, *Roll of Thunder, Hear My Cry*

2 Your journal

Throughout this book you will find that you are asked to write – not only for your teacher or for other people, but often just for yourself:

- to help you organise ideas when you're thinking about something;

- to test what the ideas and words in your head look like on paper;

- to **practise** your writing before you are asked to present it to the person or people it is written for;

- to help you decide what you want to say;

- to help you remember what you've done, or have still got to do;

- to find out what you know;

- just for fun, or relaxation;

- and, most importantly, to give you a chance to think and write about the things **you** want to write about.

This is important because your best writing will come when you write about things you're interested in, or things you've seen; and because the more opportunities you get to write, the easier writing will become.

One of the ways in which you'll have time to write for yourself will be in your **journal**.

This chapter is planned to introduce you to journal writing, and to give you a chance to find out the sorts of things you might **like** to write about, when you are free to choose.

What is a journal?

Here are some extracts from students' writing about their journals. Read their comments to yourself and jot down any questions or comments you think of as you read what they have to say.

A journal is a series of pieces of writing, usually in the form of daily entries. This writing can be of a great variety...but it is usually fairly personal and reflects the thoughts and feelings of the writer.

The aim of this is just to write for a short time each day on anything you feel like at the time. This can include...daily events and comments on these; thoughts on TV programmes, current affairs, magazine articles; reminiscences; creative writing; abstract thoughts, or any form of writing at all.

...it is also very interesting to be able to look back over the journal and see what you did and felt in the past.

JUDY

To me the journal is useful, in that I can see whether my writing is improving or not. I enjoy reading over my journal because a lot of what I wrote is interesting and tells me what I thought weeks or months ago.

A lot of the time I agree with what I thought but now and again I disagree and I can have a sort of argument with myself.

I find it easy to write in a journal because I like rattling on about things I think...I understand that some people don't seem to be able to write the journal as I do but believe this is only because they don't think. They don't try to find questions, let alone answers; they must lead very boring lives.

FIONA

I improved some of my writing and spelling. I like to write in journals because then the teacher could see what was troubling you, and what sorts of things you liked and disliked and what you did at home, where you went and she or he would have some sort of ideas what you are or do.   FRANK

My journal helps me convey my feelings. I feel I can write down just as much as I can talk. Looking back I could only write a little bit maybe 6 lines, but now I can quite easily write 2½ pages. This just expresses the fact that your journal helps out in the long run. In the beginning of the year I didn't like writing in my journal because I thought someone would read it but now I don't mind. Looking back at my spelling I can find my spelling mistakes that I couldn't find before. I didn't think my jounal played a part in me but it does. It involves me in class time and at home.
                                                           LANCE

Group work

When you've read what these students have to say about journals, spend a few minutes discussing their comments with the other people in your group. Mention any of the questions or thoughts that you may have jotted down.

● Have you ever kept a journal before? Or a diary?

● Describe that to your group if you have. What sorts of things did you write about?

● Have a think about the sorts of things you would like to write about if you had the chance.

● Who would you like to show those kinds of writing to?

You need:

- a special exercise book,
- pen or pencil,
- time to think,
- time to write,
- your teacher to help organise all of the above.

You need to know that:

- Your journal is an important part of the work you do in class;
- Regular silent writing time is likely to be given for journal writing in class;
- Your teacher will look at your journal on a regular basis (perhaps once a fortnight or once a month), but the journal will **not** be marked;
- You can write the way **you** want to, not the way someone else thinks you should;
- Your teacher will most probably keep a journal too, and will write when you write;
- If you want somebody to read and respond to your writing you can show your teacher or a friend. But the journal is not for public reading;
- If you ask your teacher to read a part of your journal, then she or he can write back to you in it;
- You can check your own writing progress in your journal, and see how your own personal style of writing develops;
- Your journal will remain your own private property at the end of the year.

A journal is **not** *a diary*

There is a difference between your journal and a diary. Here's a note from a teacher which explains that difference and also makes some suggestions about 'very private' writing.

Sometimes you may want to write about the **very** personal and private things in your life. Remember that your journal is not the same thing as a diary. In your diary, kept at home, perhaps you write the very personal thoughts you have, that no one else is to read.

Because other people might sometimes read your journal, don't write anything in it that could embarrass your group or your teacher. Be sure to avoid writing anything that they shouldn't know.

J.C.

Read through those points again so that you are very clear about what journal writing is all about.

Think again about what sorts of things you would like to write about in your journal.

Make a list of as many types of writing that you would like to try. Don't show this to anybody; you can put it inside your journal for future reference. And you can add to it whenever you want to.

Individual work – writing in your journal

Write for ten minutes without interruption. As always with your journal you may write about whatever you like.

If you're not sure, or can't think of what to write about, you might like to 'talk on paper' about what's happened during this lesson, and about your reactions and thoughts on keeping a journal. Or you might like to write down your thoughts on the new school year.

When your time is up, discuss with your group how you feel about your first journal entry.

Your teacher might organise a full class discussion so that you can hear what people in other groups think about their journals.

Whole class discussion

Some points to discuss:

1. How long do you want to spend writing your journal in class?

2. Do you wish to start with a short period of time and gradually increase the length of the silent writing time?

3. How often would you like your teacher to comment on and help you with your journals?

4. What is to be the classroom policy on writing in journals at times other than the journal-writing sessions?

5. Where will you keep your journals?

All these are important questions to discuss before the class starts to keep journals. You may find that some of the decisions you come to need to be changed from time to time during the year, or that other questions arise that need to be discussed with the whole class.

You might spend some more time now, till the end of the lesson, writing some more in your journal . . .

Who's been at the toothpaste?
I know some of you do it right
and you squeeze the tube from the bottom
and you roll up the tube as it gets used up, don't you?

But somebody
somebody here –
you know who you are
you dig your thumb in
anywhere, anyhow
and you've turned that tube of toothpaste
into a squashed sock.
You've made it so hard to use
it's like trying to get toothpaste
out of a packet of nuts.

You know who you are.
I won't ask you to come out here now
but you know who you are.

And then you went and left the top off didn't you?
So the toothpaste turned to cement.

People who do things like that should . . .
you should be ashamed of yourself.

I am.

Michael Rosen

3 The writing process: drafting and editing

You can't always go straight from an idea to a finished piece of writing in one step. Often there are lots of steps in between, and these steps are called the **writing process**. This chapter introduces you to this process. Working through all the stages in the writing process will help your writing to be as good as it possibly can be, and as suitable as you can make it for your **purpose** and **audience**.

This means that while you are working out **what** you want to say, you don't have to worry about spelling, or punctuation or getting your paragraphs right. Once your ideas are clear and organised you can then work out **how** they can best be said.

Stages of the writing process

PRE-WRITING — thinking about your purpose in writing, sorting out ideas and getting started

FIRST DRAFT — getting your ideas down on paper

REVISING — selecting the ideas that best suit your purpose, and making sure that they are clear – to yourself and to other readers

REDRAFTING — organising your ideas to suit the **form** (for example, paragraphs or stanzas); finding the right words; or sorting out a sentence

EDITING — checking on spelling and punctuation, and making sure that your ideas are still clear

PRESENTATION — preparing a final copy for sharing with your **audience**

REFLECTION — reflecting on the audience's response to your writing

Individual work

Read the introduction to this chapter over again to yourself, and then think about the stages of the writing process. If you have any problems or questions, jot them down so that you can have a whole class 'Question Time' with your teacher when everybody has finished.

1, Summer

4 kids go down to the beach.
~~of~~ 1 of them goes for a swim and is knocked over by a wave. SHe blacks at for a few seconds and when she wakes she finds she is in a different Land.

The other 3 kids think she has gone for a walk and began to get worried. They start looking for her ~~and~~ and while searching find a cave. They enter the cages ~~and~~ follow a passage and finds that it leads to a land.
This land is the same land ~~to~~ where their friend ~~is~~ ended up. after being knocked over. They discover this and ~~go~~ off on many adventure

Group work – the writing process

Here are some examples of how a piece of writing has changed from **first draft** form, through the **redrafting** process of **revising** and **editing**, to its **final form**. This writing took place when four 13-year-old girls were trying to write their own story for the other students in their class, after reading *The Lion, the Witch and the Wardrobe*. Read through these examples, and talk about them in your group.

Their **first draft** looked like this:

One of their **second drafts** was an attempt to try another idea by changing the setting:

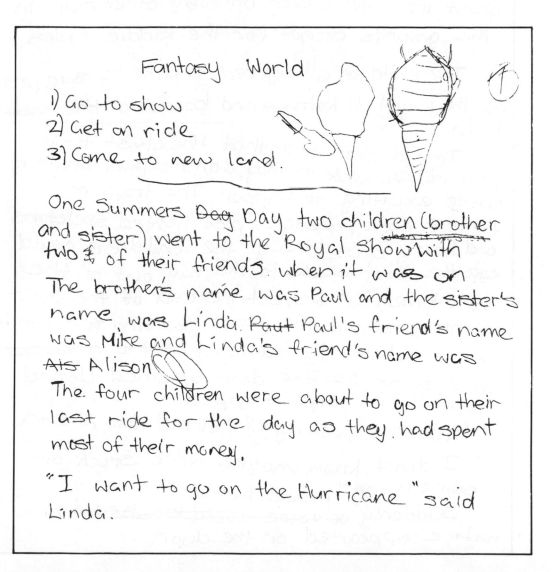

Fantasy World

1) Go to show
2) Get on ride
3) Come to new land.

One Summers ~~Day~~ Day two children (brother and ~~sister~~) went to the Royal show with two ~~£~~ of their friends. ~~when it was on~~
The brother's name was Paul and the sister's name was Linda. ~~Paul~~ Paul's friend's name was Mike and Linda's friend's name was ~~Als~~ Alison.
The four children were about to go on their last ride for the day as they had spent most of their money.

"I want to go on the Hurricane" said Linda.

"No, don't go on that. We've ~~already~~ been on it three times already "said Mike.

" Well " said Paul " I ~~suggest that we~~ want to go on a ride that we haven't been on ~~yet~~."

" Yeh so do I" said Alison.

"Alright then" ~~said~~ Mike. "Let's go on the ghost train. We've been on every other ride in the grounds except for the kiddie rides.

The children all agreed to Mike's suggestion, so they got ~~tickets~~ and boarded the ~~rid~~ train.

The children knew that the ghost train was ~~rather~~ quite weak so they didn't ~~expect~~ anything ~~exite~~ exciting to happen. The train ran through dark ~~passages~~, post lighted skeletons and hairy apes. Finally, the children could ~~see~~ the door ~~to what~~ to the way out of the dark tunnel. But ~~instead~~ instead of the door opening ~~and~~ and the train passing ~~to through~~ by it, out into the sunlight ~~The carriage stopped and an on the The~~ the door remained closed and the carriage ~~stopped~~.

" What's happening ~~?~~? "cried ~~Als~~ Alison.

" I don't know, maybe we're ~~stuck~~ or something " replied Linda.

Suddenly, ~~a voice could be heard~~ a notice appeared on the door.

However in their next draft they went back to the original idea of setting the opening of the story at the beach. As you read this extract from the **third draft**, see if you can notice anything to show that there was some use made of the discarded second draft . . .

It was a hot sunny day. Mother had suggested that Linda and Paul ask ~~some~~ their friends to go to the Beach.

Paul rang up Mike while ~~Alison~~ Linda rang up ~~Linda~~ Alison

About half an hour later Mike and ~~Linda~~ Alison arrived

Together the 4 of them walked to the beach The ~~of~~ water was a welcoming sight on ~~the~~ hot day

"Be careful of the breakers" warned Paul

"yeah they're pretty big" agreed Mike

~~Linda was the first~~

Not hearing Mike's and Paul's comment Linda was the first to enter the water.

"Hey Linda, ~~screamed~~ yelled Mike.

"Be careful!

~~it~~ Linda had not heard Mike's warning and so she turned around a huge wave was approaching her. Not being a strong swimmer Linda ~~went under~~ was knocked over.

She was tossed and turned in the swelling ~~████████████████████~~

When she surfaced she found herself somewhere never before to be seen by her eyes.

She could not focus properly, but after a few minutes she could make out the outline of men — if that was what you called them — funny men — creatures that were happy with ~~to~~ a enormously loud laugh. They were short — about 3 feet tall and their bodies — they were dumpy — not fat but dumpy.

While ~~so~~ Linda was in this strange world — cold, wet and frightened — ~~so~~ her brother and friends had begun to worry.

"Hey Mike" began Paul "did Linda get out of the water

"I don't know Paul, she's ~~st~~ probly gone for a walk. You know how she is with shells. She collects them wherever she goes

"~~Ey~~ Alison, Alison come here, we're ~~gonna~~ going to ~~start~~ looking ↑further down ~~up~~ the beach a bit. ~~around here~~ everywhere for Linda. ~~We've searched~~ ↑ and can't find her.

"Okay" answered Alison "Where do we start?"

"I think over near the caves is the place" said Paul

The three children began to ~~look for~~

Linda. They come ~~to~~ upon a cave in which Mike thought Linda might have entered.

"Lets looke in here" said Mike

The children entered the cave.

In it they found many dark passages. Cautisly they ventured up ~~a~~ one of the passages.

~~At~~ ~~the one~~ Towards the end of the passage Alison spotted light

"There's light!" ~~screamed~~ exclaimed Alison

Maybe it's the ende of this spooky cave" said Mike

Lets have a looke anyway said Paul.

The 3 ~~boys~~ ~~children~~ stepped ~~into~~ towards where the ~~could~~ light was coming from.

> Ooh look said Alison Ist
> It beautiful
>   The children couldn't
> see any of there surrounding
> clearly because their eyes were
> not accustomed to the light.
>   As their eyes adjusted
> to they could see that

The group used up many scrap pages like this one while they were writing their third draft. Once they had finished this draft they shared it with another group who read it through carefully and decided that the ideas could make a good story though they were still a bit sketchy.

The group then began to work on their **fourth draft**, remembering that in this kind of story, the writer has room to give lots of detail and description.

Their teacher pointed out that the opening chapter of a story should introduce the characters to the reader, and so the group decided to build on their third draft and add a little more conversation and detail.

Compare the opening paragraphs of the fourth draft with the beginning of the third draft to see how the writers have used conversation to make their characters seem like real people, right from the start.

> ~~Book Review - The Magic Faraway Tree~~
> _____
>   Chapter 1. red changes by
>   Jeanie.
> It was a hot, sunny day. Mother had
> suggested that Linda and Paul ask
> their friends to go to the beach.

Paul rang up Mike while Linda waited and then she rang up Alison. About half and hour later Mike and Alison arrived. Linda welcomed them and led them into the house.

"Now don't be too late" said Mrs. Ralph "I think 5.00 ~~at~~ is quite late enough."

PAD ①

"O.K, Mum" said Linda "we'll make ~~it home on time~~ sure we are home on time."

Together the four children walked to the beach. The water was a welcoming sight on the hot day.

"This'll be fun I'll be able to get some shells for my shell collection" said Linda

"Be careful of the breakers" warned Paul.

"Yeah they're pretty big" agreed ~~Paul~~ Mike.

Not having heard Mike's and
~~Paul's~~ Paul's comment, Linda ran ~~?~~ straight
to the water and plunged into the
sea.

"~~Ho~~ Hey Linda" yelled Mike
"Be careful!"

Linda turned around in the
water and saw a huge wave
approaching her. Not being a strong
swimmer Linda was knocked over
She was tossed and turned
in the swirling wave. When she
surfaced Linda found herself
~~Somewhere~~ (In a strange place) ~~where~~ she had never
~~bee~~ seen ~~be~~ before.

Finally, after all that work, the group was able to show the
fourth draft to their teacher, before **final editing**. Then they
began their final draft for **presentation** to the whole class. Here
are the first four pages:

Chapter 1

It was a hot sunny day. Mother had
suggested that Linda and Paul ask their friends to go
to the beach. Paul rang up Mike while Linda waited
and then she rang up Alison. About half an hour later,

Mike and Alison arrived. Linda welcomed them and led them into the house.

"Now! Don't be too late," said Mrs Johnson" I think 5:00 o'clock is quite late enough."

"O.K. Mum," said Linda "We'll make sure we are home on time."

Together the four children walked to the beach. The water was a welcoming sight on the hot day.

"This'll be fun! I'll be able to get some shells for my shell collection," said Linda.

"Be careful of the breakers" warned Paul

"Yeah! They're pretty big." agreed Mike.

Not having heard Mike and Paul's comments, Linda ran straight into the water and plunged into the sea.

"Hey Linda!" yelled Mike "Be careful!"

Linda turned around in the water and saw a huge wave approaching her. Not being a strong swimmer, Linda was knocked over.

She was tossed and turned in the swirling wave. When she surfaced she found herself in a strange place she had never seen before.

She could not focus properly, but, after a few minutes, she could make out the outlines of men — if that was what you called them.

The creatures that she could see had human faces, but they were only about three feet tall and their bodies were very dumpy. They had enormous loud laughs and seemed very happy.

Linda liked the little men on sight.

while she was in this strange world —
cold, wet and frightened — her brother and friends had
begun to worry.

"Hey Mike," began Paul. "Did Linda get out of the water"

"I don't know. She's probably gone for a walk. You
know how she is with shells, she collects them every
time we come down the beach."

"Alison! Alison! Have you seen Linda?" asked Paul.

"No. I thought she was in the water. Why? Where is
she?"

"We don't know. Mike and I have looked all around
here, but we can't seem to find her. I think we should
look furthur on — up the beach a bit." Paul explained.
"Will you help us look for here?"

"Sure! Where do we start?" Alison questioned.

" I think near those caves is the best place," said Mike

The three children started towards the
caves and entered the nearest one. Inside they
found many dark passages Cautiously they ventured
into one of them. Towards the end of the passage, Alison
spotted light.

"There's light!" she exclaimed.

"Maybe it's the end of this spooky tunnel." said Mike.

"Let's have a look anyway." suggested Paul.

The three children walked towards
where the light was coming from

"Look!" said Paul "there's a board with writing on it.
Let's read it. It might be important."

This is what the children read:

This is the land full of colour and light
And you have been chosen to set the scene right

The creatures they're nappy: not one of them said
But next to this land lies a land of the bad.
Witches, wizards, goblins and all
Between the two lands stands a great wall.
And over the wall in the midst of the night
Come the wizards and goblins all ready to fight.
They come from this land to conquer our mirth
They'll take all its beauty for all that its worth
Please enter this land - be not full of fright
As you're here to help us and battle our fight.

✳ ✳ ✳ ✳

All of a sudden the board disappeard and the children felt themselves being pulled towards the light by some strange force. Finally the force left them and they found that they couldn't see anything because their eyes had not accostomed to the light.

As their eyes ajusted, the children could see a huge blue lawn with funny creatures on it. "How strange," said Alison with a baffled look on her face. "Look!" exclaimed Mike "The sky – it's purple and the clouds are orange!"

"Where are we?" asked Paul.

But he recieved no answer because the creatures had spotted the three children and ran towards them. They formed into a small bunch about three metres away from the children.

You can see, even from just these extracts, that the students in this group worked very hard to make their writing as good as it could possibly be to suit their audience.

Group work

1. Read through each piece again, and see if you can find out where the changes have been made in the drafts. When you have finished, compare your ideas with those of other people in your group, so that you have tried to cover all the changes.

2. Once you have done this, spend some time thinking about **why** the authors made the changes they did. Do you think the final draft is 'better', writing than the earlier drafts? Find as many reasons as you can to say why.

3. Now share your ideas with your group, to find out what the other people thought.

Individual work

1. Look through your journal, and find a page of writing there that you think you would like to redraft to show to your teacher. You can add to it or change it in any way you like, to make it a story, or a poem, or a description.

2. When you have tried to redraft it once, give the piece a title, and then share it with one other person in your group. Ask your partner to check your writing carefully, correct any mistakes you have made, and then offer any suggestions to you.

3. Think about the suggestions for improving your writing, and then make a third draft to show to your teacher. He or she will edit that draft, and you can then make a final draft to be shared with the rest of the class.

Reflection

When you use the writing process for working on writing that is to be shared with other people, you can see that the **hard work** of revising, redrafting and editing should help your writing to improve from your first attempt.

1. Use your journal for personal reflection about the work in this chapter:

2. Do you understand the writing process better now that you have seen and practised revising and editing?

3. How did you feel when your partner corrected, criticised, or made suggestions about your writing?

4. Did you find it easy to be critical of your partner's writing?

5. Do you think that the suggestions you gave your partner were **helpful** for him or her to use for redrafting their writing?

6. Share your responses to Questions 2, 3 and 4 with your partner, and discuss together how you can be of more help to another writer next time.

4 Writing for a particular audience

This chapter is based on Jan Mark's short story 'Nothing to be Afraid Of'. It is designed to help you understand how an author's **theme** or **purpose** in telling a story is sometimes different from the story itself – from its **plot**.

In this unit you will have the chance to:

● think about the **theme** of childhood;

● talk and write about your own childhood and the things that were frightening or fun, or both;

● use Jan Mark's theme in another way, by writing for a **particular audience** – young children.

Here is Jan Mark's story. Read it through silently to yourself, and then listen as your teacher reads it to you.

Nothing to be Afraid Of
by *Jan Mark*

'Robin won't give you any trouble,' said Auntie Lynn. 'He's very quiet.'

Anthea knew how quiet Robin was. At present he was sitting under the table and, until Auntie Lynn mentioned his name, she had forgotten that he was there.

Auntie Lynn put a carrier bag on the armchair.

'There's plenty of clothes, so you won't need to do any washing, and there's a spare pair of pyjamas in case – well, you know. In case . . .'

'Yes,' said Mum, firmly. 'He'll be all right. I'll ring you tonight and let you know how he's getting along.' She looked at the clock. 'Now, hadn't *you* better be getting along?'

She saw Auntie Lynn to the front door and Anthea heard them say good-bye to each other. Mum almost told Auntie Lynn to stop worrying and have a good time, which would have been a mistake because Auntie Lynn was going up North to a funeral.

Auntie Lynn was not really an Aunt, but she had once been at school with Anthea's mum, and she was the kind of person who couldn't manage without a handle to her name; so Robin was not Anthea's cousin. Robin was not anything much, except four years old, and he looked a lot younger; probably because nothing ever happened to him. Auntie Lynn kept no pets that might give Robin germs, and never bought him toys that had sharp corners to dent him or wheels that could be swallowed. He wore balaclava helmets and bobble hats in winter to protect his tender ears, and a knitted vest under his shirt in summer in case he overheated himself and caught a chill from his own sweat.

'Perspiration,' said Auntie Lynn.

His face was as pale and flat as a saucer of milk, and his eyes floated in it like drops of cod-liver oil. This was not so surprising as he was full to the back teeth with cod-liver oil; also with extract of malt, concentrated orange juice and calves-foot jelly. When you picked him up you expected him to squelch, like a hot-water bottle full of half-set custard.

Anthea lifted the tablecloth and looked at him.

'Hello, Robin.'

Robin stared at her with his flat eyes and went back to sucking his woolly doggy that had flat eyes also, of sewn-on felt, because glass ones might find their way into Robin's appendix and cause damage. Anthea wondered how long it would be before he noticed that his mother had gone. Probably he wouldn't, any more than he would notice when she came back.

Mum closed the front door and joined Anthea in looking under the table at Robin. Robin's mouth turned down at the corners, and Anthea hoped he would cry so that they could cuddle him. It seemed impolite to cuddle him before he needed it. Anthea was afraid to go any closer.

'What a little troll,' said Mum, sadly, lowering the tablecloth. 'I suppose he'll come out when he's hungry.'

Anthea doubted it.

Robin didn't want any lunch or any tea.

'Do you think he's pining?' said Mum. Anthea did not. Anthea had a nasty suspicion that he was like this all the time. He went to bed without making a fuss and fell asleep before the light was out, as if he were too bored to stay awake. Anthea left her bedroom door open, hoping that he would have a nightmare so that she could go in and comfort him, Robin slept all night without a squeak, and woke in the morning as flat-faced as before. Wall-eyed Doggy looked more excitable than Robin did.

'If only we had a proper garden,' said Mum, as Robin went under the table again, leaving his breakfast eggs scattered round the plate. 'He might run about.'

Anthea thought that this was unlikely, and in any case they didn't have a proper garden, only a yard at the back and a stony strip in front, without a fence.

'Can I take him to the park?' said Anthea.

Mum looked doubtful. 'Do you think he wants to go?'

'No,' said Anthea, peering under the tablecloth, 'I don't think he wants to do anything, but he can't sit there all day'.'

'I bet he can,' said Mum. 'Still, I don't think he should. All right, take him to the park, but keep quiet about it. I don't suppose Lynn thinks you're safe in traffic.'

'He might tell her.'

'Can he talk?'

Robin, still clutching wall-eyed Doggy, plodded beside her all the way to the park, without once trying to jam his head between the library railings or get run over by a bus.

'Hold my hand, Robin,' Anthea said as they left the house, and he clung to her like a lamprey.

The park was not really a park at all; it was a garden. It did not even pretend to be a park and the notice by the gate said KING STREET GARDENS, in case anyone tried to use it as a park. The grass was as green and as flat as the front-room carpet, but the front-room carpet had a path worn across it from the door to the fireplace, and here there were more notices that said KEEP OFF THE GRASS, so that the gritty white paths went obediently round the edge, under the orderly trees that stood in a row like the queue outside a fish shop. There were bushes in each corner and one shelter with a bench in it. Here and there brown holes in the grass, full of raked earth, waited for next year's flowers, but there were no flowers now, and the bench had been taken out of the shelter because the shelter was supposed to be a summer-house, and you couldn't have people using a summer-house in winter.

Robin stood by the gates and gaped, with Doggy depending limply from his mouth where he held it by one ear, between his teeth. Anthea decided that if they met anyone she knew, she would explain that Robin was only two, but very big for his age.

'Do you want to run, Robin?'

Robin shook his head.

'There's nothing to be afraid of. You can go all the way round, if you like, but you mustn't walk on the grass or pick things.'

Robin nodded. It was the kind of place that he understood.

Anthea sighed. 'Well, let's walk round, then.'

They set off. At each corner, where the bushes were, the path diverged. One part went in front of the bushes, one part round the back of them. On the first circuit Robin stumped glumly beside Anthea in front of the bushes. The second time round she felt a very faint tug at her hand. Robin wanted to go his own way.

This called for a celebration. Robin could think. Anthea crouched down on the path until they were at the same level.

'You want to walk round the back of the bushes, Robin?'

'Yiss,' said Robin.

Robin could *talk*.

'All right, but listen.' She lowered her voice to a whisper. 'You must be very careful. That path is called Leopard Walk. Do you know what a leopard is?'

'Yiss.'

'There are two leopards down here. They live in the bushes. One is a good leopard and the other's a bad leopard. The good leopard has black spots. The bad leopard had red spots. If you see the bad leopard you must say, "Die leopard die or I'll kick you in the eye," and run like anything. Do you understand?'

Robin tugged again.

'Oh no,' said Anthea. 'I'm going *this* way. If you want to go down Leopard Walk, you'll have to go on your own. I'll meet you at the other end. Remember, if it's got red spots, run like mad.'

Robin trotted away. The bushes were just high enough to hide him, but Anthea could see the bobble on his hat doddering along. Suddenly the bobble gathered speed and Anthea had to run to reach the end of the bushes first.

'Did you see the bad leopard?'

'No,' said Robin, but he didn't look too sure.

'Why were you running, then?'

'I just wanted to.'

'You've dropped Doggy,' said Anthea. Doggy lay on the path with his legs in the air, halfway down Leopard Walk.

'You get him,' said Robin.

'No, *you* get him,' said Anthea. 'I'll wait here.' Robin moved off, reluctantly. She waited until he had recovered Doggy and then shouted, 'I can see the bad leopard in the bushes!' Robin raced to safety. 'Did you say, "Die leopard die or I'll kick you in the eye"?' Anthea demanded.

'No,' Robin said, guiltily.

'Then he'll *kill* us,' said Anthea. 'Come on, run. We've got to get to that tree. He can't hurt us once we're under that tree.'

They stopped running under the twisted boughs of a weeping ash. 'This is a python tree,' said Anthea. 'Look, you can see the python wound round the trunk.'

'What's a python?' said Robin, backing off.

'Oh, it's just a great big snake that squeezes people to death,' said Anthea. 'A python could easily eat a leopard. That's why leopards won't walk under this tree, you see, Robin.'

Robin looked up. 'Could it eat us?'

'Yes, but it won't if we walk on our heels.' They walked on their heels to the next corner.

'Are there leopards down there?'

'No, but we must never go down there anyway. That's Poison Alley. All the trees are poisonous. They drip poison. If one bit of poison fell on your head, you'd die.'

'I've got my hat on,' said Robin, touching the bobble to make sure.

'It would burn right through your hat,' Anthea assured him. 'Right into your brains. *Fzzzzzzz*.'

They by-passed Poison Alley and walked on over the manhole cover that clanked.

'What's that?'

'That's the Fever Pit. If anyone lifts that manhole cover, they get a terrible disease. There's this terrible disease down there, Robin, and if the lid comes off, the disease will get out and people will die. I should think there's enough disease down there to kill everybody in this town. It's ever so loose, look.'

'Don't lift it! Don't lift it!' Robin screamed, and ran to the shelter for safety.

'Don't go in there,' yelled Anthea. 'That's where the Greasy Witch lives.' Robin bounced out of the shelter as though he were on elastic.

'Where's the Greasy Witch?'

'Oh, you can't see her,' said Anthea, 'but you can tell where she is because she smells so horrible. I think she must be somewhere about. Can't you smell her now?'

Robin sniffed the air and clasped Doggy more tightly.

'And she leaves oily marks wherever she goes. Look, you can see them on the wall.'

Robin looked at the wall. Someone had been very busy, if not the Greasy Witch. Anthea was glad on the whole that Robin could not read.

'The smell's getting worse, isn't it, Robin? I think we'd better go down here and then she won't find us.'

'She'll see us.'

'No, she won't. She can't see with her eyes because they're full of grease. She sees with her ears, but I expect they're all waxy. She's a filthy old witch, really.'

They slipped down a secret-looking path that went round the back of the shelter.

'Is the Greasy Witch down here?' said Robin, fearfully.

'I don't known,' said Anthea. 'Let's investigate.' They tiptoed round the side of the shelter. The path was damp and slippery. 'Filthy old witch. She's certainly *been* here,' said Anthea. 'I think she's gone now. I'll just have a look.'

She craned her neck round the corner of the shelter. There was a sort of glade in the bushes, and in the middle was a stand-pipe, with a tap on top. The pipe was lagged with canvas, like a scaly skin.

'Frightful Corner,' said Anthea. Robin put his cautious head round the edge of the shelter.

'What's that?'

Anthea wondered if it could be a dragon, up on the tip of its tail and ready to strike, but on the other side of the bushes was the brick back wall of the King Street Public Conveniences, and at that moment she heard the unmistakable sound of a cistern flushing.

'It's a Lavatory Demon,' she said. 'Quick! We've got to get away before the water stops, or he'll have us.'

They ran all the way to the gates, where they could see the church clock, and it was almost time for lunch.

Auntie Lynn fetched Robin home next morning, and three days later she was back again, striding up the path like warrior queen going into battle, with Robin dangling from her hand, and Doggy dangling from Robin's hand.

Mum took her into the front room, closing the door. Anthea sat on the stairs and listened. Auntie Lynn was in full throat and furious, so it was easy enough to hear what she had to say.

'I want a word with that young lady,' said Auntie Lynn. 'And I want to know what she's been telling him.' Her voice dropped, and Anthea could hear only certain fateful words: 'Leopards . . . poison trees . . . snakes . . . diseases!'

Mum said something very quietly that Anthea did not hear, and then Auntie Lynn turned up the volume once more.

'Won't go to bed unless I leave the door open . . . wants the light on . . . up and down to him all night . . . won't go the bathroom on his own. He says the – the – ,' she hesitated, 'the *toilet* demons will get him. He nearly broke his neck running downstairs this morning.'

Mum spoke again, but Auntie Lynn cut in like a band-saw.

'Frightened out of his wits! He follows me everywhere.'

The door opened slightly, and Anthea got ready to bolt, but it was Robin who came out, with his thumb in his mouth and circles round his eyes. Under his arm was soggy Doggy, ears chewed to nervous rags.

Robin looked up at Anthea through the banisters.

'Let's go to the park,' he said.

This is a story that doesn't really have a 'plot' like some of the other short stories you will have read. Jan Mark has just written about one afternoon's outing to a park.

Group work

1. Jot down some notes for yourself about the story – any clues or ideas you have that might help answer the question: What was the author trying to say in this story? Or, what does the story do for the reader? Your jottings might include notes of things that puzzle you, parts you liked, and things, people or events that the story reminds you of.

2. When your group has had time to write some notes, spend ten minutes talking about the story to share each other's ideas and memories. Jot down any new ideas you might have.

3. When you have heard all the ideas of your group, use your own notes to write a statement on what you think the story is about, and what you think the author is really trying to say.

4. Your presentation copies could be pinned up, or shared around the class before they are collected, so that you can compare your ideas with those of other people in your class.

5. In your group, talk about what could have happened when Auntie Lynn sees Anthea. Does Robin ever go to the park again?

6. Talk with each other about some of the incidents in your own childhood that you remember clearly. Have any other children in your family had any 'important' adventures?

Individual work

As a longer project, you might like to use the ideas from this story, and the work you have done, to write a story for a young child about him or herself.

Read through the following guidelines carefully, and plan with your teacher how much time you have to do this project, and how you will organise yourself.

1. Arrange with your teacher to visit an infant class at a nearby school.

    You'll probably have to write to the class teacher at the school, saying what times you could visit the class, and explaining that you want to talk to one of the children for this project.

2. When the visit is organised, you will have to explain to 'your' child what you are doing, and ask him or her to tell you something about themselves that you could turn into a story.

    You will need to plan some questions to ask. If your child is a bit shy, it might be a good idea to start by telling some stories about yourself or a classmate.

    You could make a tape-recording or take notes as you go.

3. After you have collected some ideas for a story, you will have to talk with your child's teacher to make sure you know what sorts of books he or she can read.

    Have a look at some of the books in the classroom, and ask your child what sorts he or she likes best.

4. Then you can go about turning the 'adventure' into a real book.

    When you write the story you will be the narrator, describing the events from a distance. You will be writing in the **third person**, referring to your child by name, and as 'he' or 'she'.

5. Work on your story with the help of your group members and your teacher. You could do your own drawings, or cut pictures from magazines to illustrate the story. When the pages are in book form, you can design a cover to go on the front, then arrange to visit your child again so you can present the book. Ask your teacher to make a photocopy for you to keep first.

Note: This project can, of course, be adapted to make books for children in hospital, or your own younger brothers or sisters, cousins, nephews, nieces – anyone you like!

Reflection

When you've finished the work on this project, spend some time thinking and talking about what you did and what you learnt:

- about writing for a particular audience – in this case a young child,

- about how authors can convey an idea or theme through a story,

- about the difference between first and third person narration,

- about other stories that this reminds you of, and about how what you have been doing fits in with the other work you have done this year.

Make a journal entry for your teacher giving some of your thoughts about this project.

5 Creating suspense

This chapter gives you the opportunity to look closely at a short story and a poem so that you can learn something about the way in which the authors have created suspense in their writing. You should be able to apply some of what you learn to your own writing.

In the first three paragraphs of 'Spit Nolan', the author prepares us for what will happen in this short story. Read the introduction carefully to yourself.

Spit Nolan
by *Bill Naughton*

Spit Nolan was a pal of mine. He was a thin lad with a bony face that was always pale, except for two rosy spots on his cheekbones. He had quick brown eyes, short, wiry hair, rather stooped shoulders, and we all knew that he had only one lung. He had a disease which in those days couldn't be cured unless you went away to Switzerland, which Spit certainly couldn't afford. He wasn't sorry for himself in any way, and in fact we envied him, because he never had to go to school.

Spit was the champion trolley-rider of Cotton Pocket; that was the district in which we lived. He had a very good balance, and sharp wits, and he was very brave, so that these qualities, when added to his skill as a rider, meant that no other boy could ever beat Spit on a trolley – and every lad had one.

Our trolleys were simple vehicles for getting a good ride downhill at a fast speed. To make one you had to get a stout piece of wood about five feet in length and eighteen inches wide. Then you needed four wheels, preferably two pairs, large ones for the back and smaller ones for the front. However, since we bought our wheels from the scrapyard, most trolleys had four odd wheels. Now you had to get a poker and put it in the fire until it was red hot, and then burn a hole through the wood at the front. Usually it would take three or four attempts to get the hole bored through. Through this hole you fitted the giant nut-and-bolt, which acted as a swivel for the steering. Fastened to the nut was a strip of wood, on to which the front axle was secured by bent nails. A piece of rope tied to each end of the axle served for steering. Then a knob of margarine had to be slanced out of the kitchen to grease the wheels and bearings. Next you had to paint a name on it: *Invincible* or *Dreadnought*, though it might be a motto: *Death before Dishonour* or *Labour and Wait*. That done, you then stuck your chest out, opened the back gate, and wheeled your trolley out to face the critical eyes of the world.

Individual and group work – exploration

1. Go over in your mind the things you know about Spit Nolan.

2. Share your thoughts with the people in your group to see if you came to the same conclusions.

3. Read the paragraphs again, and think about how you would **continue** this story.

4. Write the first draft of **your** story about Spit Nolan, without looking at the rest of Bill Naughton's story.

It is important that you maintain the **point of view** which Bill Naughton has established in the first two paragraphs.

Who is telling the story?

Is it written in the first person or in the third person?

Check with your teacher to see you fully understand this before you begin writing your story.

5. When you have finished your first draft, exchange it with the others in your group, to see what sort of stories you have made, and explain why you chose to tell the story you did.

6. You might like to redraft your story later, to share with another group, or with your teacher, when you are satisfied with it as a final product. But once you have completed the first draft continue with the rest of the chapter.

Here is how Bill Naughton finished his story about Spit Nolan:

Spit spent most mornings trying out new speed gadgets on his trolley, or searching Enty's scrapyard for good wheels. Afternoons he would go off and have a spin down Cemetery Brew. This was a very steep road that led to the cemetery, and it was very popular with trolley-drivers as it was the only macadamised hill for miles around, all the others being cobblestones for horse traffic.

Spit used to lie in wait for a coal-cart or other horse-drawn vehicle, then he would hitch *Egdam* to the back to take it up the brew.

Egdam was a name in memory of a girl called Madge, whom he had once met at Southport Sanatorium, where he had spent three happy weeks. Only I knew the meaning of it, for he had reversed the letters of her name to keep his love a secret.

It was the custom for lads to gather at the street corner on summer evenings and, trolleys parked at hand, discuss trolleying, road surfaces, and also show off any new gadgets. Then, when Spit gave the sign, we used to set off for Cemetery Brew. There was scarcely any evening traffic on the roads in those days, so that we could have a good practice before our evening race. Spit, the unbeaten champion, would inspect every trolley and rider, and allow a start which was reckoned on the size of the wheels and the weight of the rider. He was always the last in the line of starters, though no matter how long a start he gave it seemed impossible to beat him. He knew that road like the palm of his hand, every tiny lump or pothole, and he never came a cropper.

Among us he took things easy, but when occasion asked for it he would go all out. Once he had to meet a challenge from Ducker Smith, the champion of the Engine Row gang. On that occasion Spit borrowed a wheel from the baby's pram, removing one nearest the wall, so it wouldn't be missed, and confident he could replace it before his mother took baby out. And after fixing it to his trolley he made that ride in what was called the 'belly-down' style — that is, he lay full stretch on his stomach, so as to avoid wind resistance. Although Ducker got away with a flying start he had not that sensitive touch of Spit, and his frequent bumps and swerves lost him valuable inches, so that he lost the race with a good three lengths. Spit arrived home just in time to catch his mother as she was wheeling young Georgie off the doorstep, and if he had not made a dash for it the child would have fallen out as the pram overturned.

It happened that we were gathered at the street corner with our trolleys one evening when Ernie Haddock let out a hiccup of wonder: 'Hy, chaps, wot's Leslie got?'

We all turned our eyes on Leslie Duckett, the plump son of the local publican. He approached us on a brand-new trolley, propelled by flicks of his foot on the pavement. From a distance the thing had looked impressive, but now, when it came up among us, we were too dumbfounded to speak. Such a magnificent trolley had never been seen! The riding board was of solid oak, almost two inches thick; four new wheels with pneumatic tyres; a brake, a bell, a lamp, and a spotless steering-cord. In front was a plate on which was the name in bold lettering: *The British Queen*.

'It's called after the pub,' remarked Leslie. He tried to edge it away from Spit's trolley, for it made *Egdam* appear horribly insignificant. Voices had been stilled for a minute, but now they broke out:

'Where'd it come from?'

'How much was it?'

'Who made it?'

Leslie tried to look modest. 'My dad had it specially made to measure,' he said, 'by the gaffer of the Holt Engineering Works.'

He was a nice lad, and now he wasn't sure whether to feel proud or ashamed. The fact was, nobody had ever had a trolley made by somebody else. Trolleys were swopped and so on, but no lad had ever owned one that had been made by other hands. We went quiet now, for Spit had calmly turned his attention to it, and was examining *The British Queen* with his expert eye. First he tilted it, so that one of the rear wheels was off the ground, and after giving it a flick of the finger he listened intently with his ear close to the hub.

'A beautiful ball-bearing race,' he remarked, 'it runs like silk.' Next he turned his attention to the body. 'Grand piece of timber, Leslie – though a trifle on the heavy side. It'll take plenty of pulling up a brew.'

'I can pull it,' said Leslie, stiffening.

'You might find it a shade *front-heavy*,' went on Spit, 'which means it'll be hard on the steering unless you keep it well oiled.'

'It's well made,' said Leslie. 'Eh, Spit?'

Spit nodded. 'Aye, all the bolts are counter sunk,' he said, 'everything chamfered and fluted off to perfection. But – '

'But what?' asked Leslie.

'Do you want me to tell you?' asked Spit.

'Yes, I do,' answered Leslie.

'Well, it's got none of *you* in it,' said Spit.

'How do you mean?' says Leslie.

'Well, you haven't so much as given it a single tap with a hammer,' said Spit. 'That trolley will be a stranger to you to your dying day.'

'How come,' said Leslie, 'since I *own* it?'

Spit shook his head. 'You don't own it,' he said, in a quiet, solemn tone. 'You own nothing in this world except those things you have taken a hand in the making of, or else you've earned the money to buy them.'

Leslie sat down on *The British Queen* to think this one out. We all sat around, scratching our heads.

'You've forgotten to mention one thing,' said Ernie Haddock to Spit, 'what about the *speed*?'

'Going down a steep hill,' said Spit, 'she should hold the road well – an' with wheels like that she should certainly be able to shift some.'

'Think she could beat *Egdam*?' ventured Ernie.

'That,' said Spit, 'remains to be seen.'

Ernie gave a shout: 'A challenge race! *The British Queen* versus *Egdam*!'

'Not tonight,' said Leslie. 'I haven't got the proper feel of her yet.'

'What about Sunday morning?' I said.

Spit nodded. 'As good a time as any.'

Leslie agreed. 'By then,' he said in a challenging tone, 'I'll be able to handle her.'

Chattering like monkeys, eating bread, carrots, fruit, and bits of toffee, the entire gang of us made our way along the silent Sunday-morning streets for the big race at Cemetery Brew. We were split into two fairly equal sides.

Leslie, in his serge Sunday suit, walked ahead, with Ernie Haddock pulling *The British Queen*, and a bunch of supporters around. They were optimistic, for Leslie had easily outpaced every other trolley during the week, though as yet he had not run against Spit.

Spit was in the middle of the group behind, and I was pulling *Egdam* and keeping the pace easy, for I wanted Spit to keep fresh. He walked in and out among us with an air of imperturbability that, considering the occasion, seemed almost godlike. It inspired a fanatical confidence in us. It was such that Chick Dale, a curly-headed kid with soft skin like a girl's, and a nervous lisp, climbed up on to the spiked railing of the cemetery, and, reaching out with his thin fingers, snatched a yellow rose. He ran in front of Spit and thrust it into a small hole in his jersey:

'I pwesent you with the wose of the winner!' he exclaimed.

'And I've a good mind to present you with a clout on the lug,' replied Spit, 'for pinching a flower from a cemetery. An' what's more, it's bad luck.' Seeing Chick's face, he relented. 'On second thoughts, Chick, I'll wear it. Ee, wot a 'eavenly smell!'

Happily we went along, and Spit turned to a couple of lads at the back. 'Hy, stop that whistling. Don't forget what day it is – folk want their sleep out.'

A faint sweated glow had come over Spit's face when we reached the top of the hill, but he was as majestically calm as ever. Taking the bottle of cold water from his trolley seat, he put it to his lips and rinsed out his mouth in the manner of a boxer.

The two contestants were called together by Ernie.

'No bumpin' or borin',' he said.

They nodded.

'The winner,' he said, 'is the first who puts the nose of his trolley past the cemetery gates.'

They nodded.

'Now, who,' he asked, 'is to be judge?'

Leslie looked at me. 'I've no objection to Bill,' he said. 'I know he's straight.'

I hadn't realised I was, I thought, but by heck I will be!

'Ernie here,' said Spit, 'can be starter.'

With that Leslie and Spit shook hands.

'Fly down to them gates,' said Ernie to me. He had his father's pigeon-timing watch in his hand. 'I'll be setting 'em off dead on the stroke of ten o'clock.'

I hurried down to the gates. I looked back and saw the supporters lining themselves on either side of the road. Leslie was sitting upright on *The British Queen.* Spit was settling himself to ride belly-down. Ernie Haddock, handkerchief raised in the right hand, eye gazing down on the watch in the left, was counting them off – just like when he tossed one of his father's pigeons.

'Five – four – three – two – one – *Off!*'

Spit was away like a shot. That vigorous toe push sent him clean ahead of Leslie. A volley of shouts went up from his supporters, and groans from Leslie's. I saw Spit move straight to the middle of the road camber. Then I ran ahead to take up my position at the winning post.

When I turned again I was surprised to see that Spit had not increased the lead. In fact, it seemed that Leslie had begun to gain on him. He had settled himself into a crouched position, and those perfect wheels combined with his extra weight were bringing him up with Spit. Not that it seemed possible he could ever catch him. For Spit, lying flat on his trolley, moving with a fine balance, gliding, as it were, over the rough patches, looked to me as though he were a bird that might suddenly open out its wings and fly clean in to the air.

The runners along the side could no longer keep up with the trolleys. And now, as they skimmed past the half-way mark, and came to the very steepest part, there was no doubt that Leslie was gaining. Spit had never ridden better; he coaxed *Egdam* over the tricky parts, swayed with her, gave her her head, and guided her. Yet Leslie, clinging grimly to the steering-rope of *The British Queen*, and riding the rougher part of the road, was actually drawing level. Those beautiful ball-bearing wheels, engineer-made, encased in oil, were holding the road, and bringing Leslie along faster than spirit and skill could carry Spit.

Dead level they sped into the final stretch. Spit's slight figure was poised fearlessly on his trolley, drawing the extremes of speed from her. Thundering beside him, anxious but determined, came Leslie. He was actually drawing ahead – and forcing his way to the top of the camber. On they came like two charioteers – Spit delicately edging to the side, to gain inches by the extra downward momentum. I kept my eyes fastened clean across the road as they came belting past the winning-post.

First past was the plate *The British Queen*. I saw that first. Then I saw the heavy rear wheel jog over a pothole and strike Spit's front wheel – sending him in a swerve across the road. Suddenly then, from nowhere, a charabanc came speeding round the wide bend.

Spit was straight in its path. Nothing could avoid the collision. I gave a cry of fear as I saw the heavy solid tyre of the front wheel hit the trolley. Spit was flung up and his back hit the radiator. Then the driver stopped dead.

I got there first. Spit was lying on the macadam road on his side. His face was white and dusty, and coming out between his lips and trickling down his chin was a rivulet of fresh red blood. Scattered all about him were yellow rose petals.

'Not my fault,' I heard the driver shouting. 'I didn't have a chance. He came straight at me.'

The next thing we were surrounded by women who had got out of the charabanc. And then Leslie and all the lads came up.

'Somebody send for an ambulance!' called a woman.

'I'll run an' tell the gatekeeper to telephone,' said Ernie Haddock.

'I hadn't a chance,' the driver explained to the women.

'A piece of his jersey on the starting-handle there . . .' said someone.

'Don't move him,' said the driver to a stout woman who had bent over Spit. 'Wait for the ambulance.'

'Hush up,' she said. She knelt and put a silk scarf under Spit's head. Then she wiped his mouth with her little handkerchief.

He opened his eyes. Glazed they were, as though he couldn't see. A short cough came out of him, then he looked at me and his lips moved.

'*Who won?*'

'Thee!' blurted out Leslie. 'Tha just licked me. Eh, Bill?'

'Aye,' I said, 'old *Egdam* just pipped *The British Queen*.'

Spit's eyes closed again. The women looked at each other. They nearly all had tears in their eyes. Then Spit looked up again, and his wise, knowing look came over his face. After a minute he spoke in a sharp whisper:

'Liars. I can remember seeing Leslie's back wheel hit my front 'un. I didn't win – I lost.' He stared upward for a few seconds, then his eyes twitched and shut.

The driver kept repeating how it wasn't his fault, and next thing the ambulance came. Nearly all the women were crying now, and I saw the look that went between the two men who put Spit on a stretcher – but I couldn't believe he was dead. I had to go into the ambulance with the attendant to give him particulars. I went up the step and sat down inside and looked out the little window as the driver slammed the doors. I saw the driver holding Leslie as a witness. Chick Dale was lifting the smashed-up *Egdam* on to the body of *The British Queen*. People with bunches of flowers in their hands stared after us as we drove off. Then I heard the ambulance man asking me Spit's name. Then he touched me on the elbow with his pencil and said:

'Where *did* he live?'

I knew then. That word 'did' struck right into me. But for a minute I couldn't answer. I had to think hard, for the way he said it made it suddenly seem as thought Spit Nolan had been dead and gone for ages.

Group work – exploring the story

1. Did Spit's death come as a shock to you, or did you expect it? Do you feel sad about Spit's death? Talk about these questions in your group for a few minutes, to see what the other people thought and felt.

2. Then look back at the **first two paragraphs** again.

   ● Is there anything in them that you can now see might be a clue that Bill Naughton was going to write about Spit's death?

   ● Did anybody in your group write a story in which Spit died?

   ● Discuss the similarities and the differences between the stories you wrote and Bill Naughton's story. You might like to share your ideas with the rest of the class to see what other people wrote.

3. Now go carefully through 'Spit Nolan', looking for all the hints that Bill Naughton gives to prepare us for Spit's death. Write

these down for yourselves, and check with your group if you are uncertain about any of them.

4. As a large group, discuss the reason why you feel Bill Naughton rejected a 'Hollywood-film' ending with Spit dying happily thinking he had won the race.

5. 'You own nothing in this world except those things you have taken a hand in the making of, or else you've earned the money to buy them.'
   You might like to copy this quotation into your journal so that you can write your thoughts about it later.

The Highwayman

PART ONE

The wind was a torrent of darkness among the gusty trees,
The moon was a ghostly galleon tossed upon cloudy seas,
The road was a ribbon of moonlight over the purple moor,
And the highwayman came riding –
    Riding – riding –
The highwayman came riding, up to the old inn-door.
He'd a French cocked-hat on his forehead, a bunch of lace
    at his chin,
A coat of the claret velvet, and breeches of brown doeskin:
They fitted with never a wrinkle; his boots were up to the thigh!

And he rode with a jewelled twinkle,
    His pistol butts a-twinkle,
His rapier hilt a-twinkle, under the jewelled sky.

Over the cobbles he clattered and clashed in the dark inn-yard,
And he tapped with his whip on the shutters, but all was locked
    and barred:
He whistled a tune to the window; and who should be waiting
    there
But the landlord's black-eyed daughter,

Bess, the landlord's daughter,
Plaiting a dark red love-knot into her long black hair.

And dark in the dark old inn-yard a stable-wicket creaked
Where Tim, the ostler, listened; his face was white and peaked,
His eyes were hollows of madness, his hair like mouldy hay;
But he loved the landlord's daughter,
    The landlord's red-lipped daughter:
Dumb as a dog he listened, and he heard the robber say –

'One kiss, my bonny sweetheart, I'm after a prize tonight,
But I shall be back with the yellow gold before the morning light.
Yet if they press me sharply, and harry me through the day,
Then look for me by moonlight,
    Watch for me by moonlight:
I'll come to thee by moonlight, though Hell should bar the way.'

He rose upright in the stirrups, he scarce could reach her hand;
But she loosened her hair i'the casement! His face burnt like a
        brand
As the black cascade of perfume came tumbling over his breast;
And he kissed its waves in the moonlight,
    (Oh, sweet black waves in the moonlight)
Then he tugged at his reins in the moonlight, and galloped away
        to the West.

PART TWO

He did not come in the dawning; he did not come at noon;
And out of the tawny sunset, before the rise o' the moon,
When the road was a gypsy's ribbon, looping the purple moor,
A red-coat troop came marching –
    Marching – marching –
King George's men came marching, up to the old inn-door.

They said no word to the landlord, they drank his ale instead;
But they gagged his daughter and bound her to the foot of her
        narrow bed.
Two of them knelt at her casement, with muskets at the side!
There was death at every window;
    And Hell at one dark window;
For Bess could see, through her casement, the road that *he*
        would ride.

They had tied her up to attention, with many a sniggering jest:
They had bound a musket beside her, with the barrel beneath
    her breast!
'Now keep good watch!' and they kissed her.
   She heard the dead man say –
Look for me by moonlight;
   Watch for me by moonlight;
I'll come to thee by moonlight, though Hell should bar the way!

She twisted her hands behind her; but all the knots held good!
She writhed her hands till her fingers were wet with sweat or
    blood!
They stretched and strained in the darkness, and the hours
    crawled by like years;
Till, now, on the stroke of midnight,
   Cold, on the stroke of midnight,
The tip of one finger touched it! The trigger at least was hers!

The tip of one finger touched it; she strove no more for the rest!
Up, she stood up to attention, with the barrel beneath her breast,
She would not risk their hearing: she would not strive again;
For the road lay bare in the moonlight,
   Blank and bare in the moonlight;
And the blood in her veins in the moonlight throbbed to her
    Love's refrain.

Tlot-tlot, tlot-tlot! Had they heard it? The horse-hoofs ringing
    clear –
Tlot-tlot, tlot-tlot, in the distance? Were they deaf that they did
    not hear?
Down the ribbon of moonlight, over the brow of the hill,
The highwayman came riding,
   Riding, riding!
The red-coats looked to their priming! She stood up straight and
    still!

Tlot-tlot, in the frosty silence! *Tlot-tlot* in the echoing night!
Nearer he came and nearer! Her face was like a light!
Her eyes grew wide for a moment; she drew one last deep breath,
Then her finger moved in the moonlight,
   Her musket shattered the moonlight,
Shattered her breast in the moonlight and warned him – with
    her death.

He turned; he spurred him westward; he did not know who stood
Bowed with her head o'er the musket, drenched with her own
    red blood!
Not till the dawn he heard it, and slowly blanched to hear
How Bess, the landlord's daughter,
    The landlord's black-eyed daughter,
Had watched for her Love in the moonlight; and died in the
    darkness there.

Back, he spurred like a madman, shrieking a curse to the sky,
With the white road smoking behind him, and his rapier
    brandished high!

Blood-red were his spurs i'the golden noon; wine-red was his
    velvet coat;
When they shot him down on the highway,
    Down like a dog on the highway,
And he lay in his blood on the highway, with the bunch of lace at
    his throat.

And still of a winter's night, they say, when the wind is in the trees,
When the moon is a ghostly galleon tossed upon cloudy seas,
When the road is a ribbon of moonlight over the purple moor,
A highwayman comes riding –
    Riding – riding –
A highwayman comes riding, up to the old inn-door.

Over the cobbles he clatters and clangs in the dark inn-yard;
And he taps with his whip on the shutters, but all is locked and
    barred:
He whistles a tune to the window, and who should be waiting there
But the landlord's black-eyed daughter,
    Bess, the landlord's daughter,
Plaiting a dark red love-knot into her long black hair.

                                                        Alfred Noyes

Group work – exploring the poem

Reading

After your teacher has read the poem aloud, read it through silently to yourself to try to understand it more clearly. Try to **hear** it in your head as you read.

It is a very good poem to read aloud so try this within your group. Use your imagination in breaking the poem into parts for different members of your group to read. Some of the groups may be prepared to read the poem aloud to the whole class.

Talking

To make sure that you understand the poem:

- retell the story within your group.

- tell your teacher how the soldiers knew that the highwayman would be visiting the Inn.

Whole class work – metaphors in 'The Highwayman'

To fully appreciate the poem it is worth looking closely at the descriptions of:

- the setting,

- the highwayman,

- Tim, the ostler,

- the highwayman's death.

Because Alfred Noyes wants to make his descriptions both vivid and concise, he uses many **metaphors** in 'The Highwayman'. A **metaphor** is a figure of speech in which two objects are compared. When the poet says 'The wind was a torrent of darkness', he is comparing the wind to a 'torrent of darkness' because he wants to suggest the darkness of the scene and the force of the wind. He reinforces this idea with another metaphor describing the moon as a ghostly galleon tossed upon cloudy seas. Think about this line and see what pictures these metaphors bring to your mind.

The following examples might remind you that we use metaphors all the time in our own conversations:

'The night was pitch black.'
'He let out a torrent of abuse.'
'She made a cutting remark.'
'The detective smelt a rat.'

One thing worth noting is the difference between **metaphors** and **similes**. A simile is a comparison which involves the words 'as' or 'like'. For example; *his hair like mouldy hay* and *Dumb as a dog he listened* are similes.

Group work

1. Each group member should write down a list of as many examples as possible of metaphors which they use from time to time in conversation.

2. Make up a group list of the best metaphors from your individual lists. Share these with the whole class.

3. Look at Alfred Noyes' use of metaphor in his description of:

● the setting of the poem,

● the highwayman,

● Tim, the ostler.

4. Now look at the poet's use of similes throughout the poem.

5. In completing questions 3 and 4 you will firstly have to find the metaphors and similes. Then you must try to say what effect the metaphors or similes have on you. When the poet says, 'He rode with a jewelled twinkle', what do you imagine? How does this picture affect how you feel about the highwayman?

6. Your teacher will organise for you to move to new groups with one student from each of three or four different groups. Exchange your findings. As a group decide which metaphors and similes you found most effective. Report back to the class on this.

Additional activities

Drama

'The Highwayman' lends itself to a number of dramatic activities which you will not only enjoy but which also should help you to understand and appreciate the poem more. Working in your groups, decide how you would like to adapt the poem to a dramatic performance.

● Will you perform the whole poem or just scenes from it?

● How will you link the scenes?

● How much of the poem itself will you use?

● Will you add any extra scenes that aren't in the poem?

Writing – point of view in 'The Highwayman'

1. Tell the story from the **point of view** of one of the following:

● Tim, the ostler,

● Bess's father, the landlord,

● one of the red-coat soldiers.

Imagine that you are one of these characters telling the story a day, or a week, or a year after the death of the highwayman. Notice that **when** you tell the story may influence how you feel about the events.

2. You may wish to look at the events through the eyes of either Bess or the highwayman. In this case you could recount Bess's thoughts as she waits, tied up with her finger on the trigger of the musket, for her highwayman to return. If you wish to look at the story through the eyes of the highwayman you could describe his thoughts as he rides back to the inn at noon.

3. Another possibility would be to recount the conversation of the red-coat troop after they arrive at the inn to wait for the highwayman, or after Bess kills herself, or at another inn a week after they've shot the highwayman.

4. Try to select four different possibilities within your group so that you can see how different the story is when it is seen from different points of view. You may also wish to exchange your stories with other groups in the class to see how they've tackled the subject.

Whole class work – suspense

These activities are designed to show how **suspense** can be built up so that you can use some of the techniques in your own writing when you need to.

Suspense is a vital element in the plot of nearly all novels, short stories, plays or films. Suspense arises because we are in doubt about how the story will end. The writer controls the story so that the readers are uncertain about what will happen. Two main techniques which writers use to create suspense are:

● to arouse our curiosity and not satisfy it immediately,

● to hint about future events.

1. Think about recent films and television shows that you've seen. Make a group list of as many examples as you can think of to show how a feeling of suspense was created.

2. Arrange for each group to watch a different TV programme during the week, taking notes on how suspense is built up during the show.

● Report to the rest of the class on your findings, and then hold a class discussion on the similarities and differences in the techniques used in different programmes.

● Make up a class list of all the techniques you have discussed.

3. Discuss with the rest of your group how you could use these techniques in your writing.

Group work – suspense

Your teacher will divide the class into A Groups (to look at 'Spit Nolan') and B Groups (to look at 'The Highwayman'). In these groups you will look at how suspense is built up in either the story or the poem.

1. Look at either the story or the poem and make a list of examples of how the writer builds up suspense.

2. Your teacher will help you to form **new groups** with two students from an A Group joining with two from a B Group. You will all need your notes from the previous activity. Those who looked at 'Spit Nolan' should explain the examples of suspense in that story and then the students who examined 'The Highwayman' should describe the build-up of suspense in the poem.

3. From these examples, and from the work you did on films and television shows can you make a list of **techniques of suspense**. Two techniques mentioned earlier were:

● to arouse our curiosity and not satisfy it,

● to hint about future events.

Which examples from the story and the poem used these techniques? What other techniques can be used?

4. Now, from your group lists, make up a class list of **techniques of suspense**.

Individual work – writing a story

You might like to write about a real event in your own life, where something came as a shock to you. Try to make your readers feel the same sort of surprise or shock, by using some of the techniques you have discussed in this chapter.

You could try your hand at using some of the techniques of suspense you've learned about in writing a story to entertain or scare or puzzle your readers. You could try: an adventure story; a ghost story; a murder story; a mystery story.

A suggested approach

1. Decide on **how you'll tell your story**. You may choose to narrate it in a similar way to Bill Naughton in 'Spit Nolan' where the story is told in the first person by someone who is not the main character. Discuss this with your teacher.

2. Decide on the **setting** of your story. Where and when will it take place?

3. Make a rough plan or outline of the **plot**. What happens?

4. What **techniques of suspense** will you use? At what points in the story will you introduce suspense?

5. Start on your **first draft**.

6. When you've finished your first draft, share it with another person in your group. Discuss how you could improve your story before you **revise** and **edit**.

7. The **final drafts**, of all the stories the class has written could be collected into a book for the class library, or displayed on the notice board so that everybody can read them; so check with your group and your teacher for editing, before you write your final draft.

Reflection

Do you think that what you have learnt about techniques of creating suspense in writing will help you tell and write better stories in the future?

Did you find any other techniques while you were writing your own story? If you did, add these to the list you have made.

You might be interested in some other novels, short stories and poems that build up suspense. Ask your teacher or your librarian about books such as these:

Joan Aiken, *The Wolves of Willoughby Chase*

Peter Dickinson, *Annerton Pit*

Leon Garfield, *Black Jack*

John Gordon, *Giant under the Snow*

Alfred Hitchcock, *Sinister Spies*

Alfred Hitchcock, *The Haunted Houseful*

William Mayne, *Earthfasts*

Edgar Alan Poe, *Eight Tales of Terror*

6 Ballads

This chapter looks at a popular form of telling stories in verse – the ballad. By looking at some well-known British, American and Australian ballads you will learn about some of the techniques that the composers of ballads have used.

Because ballads come from an **oral** tradition, many of the activities in this chapter are oral. You will be involved in reading aloud, choral speaking and drama.

For the teacher   The first three ballads in this chapter are included for students to experience and enjoy. You might begin the chapter by playing recordings of these ballads or by singing or reading these to the class before focusing on 'The Raggle Taggle Gypsies'.

Ten Thousand Miles Away

Sing ho, for a brave and gallant ship
And a fair and fav'ring breeze,
With a bully crew and a captain too
To carry me over seas,
To carry me over seas, my boys,
To my true love far away;
I'm taking a trip on a gov'ment ship,
Ten thousand miles away

Then blow ye winds heigh-ho! A-roving I will go,
I'll stay no more on England's shore
To hear the music play,
I'm off on the morning train to cross the raging main,
I'm taking a trip on a gov'ment ship,
Ten thousand miles away.

My true love she was beautiful,
My true love she was young,
Her eyes were like the diamonds bright,
And silvery was her tongue, my boys,
Though she's far away –
She's taken a trip on a gov'ment ship
Ten thousand miles away.

Oh, dark and dismal was the day
When last I seen my Meg;
She'd a gov'ment band around each hand,
And another one round her leg;
And another one round her leg, my boys,
As the big ship left the bay –
'Adieu,' said she, 'remember me,
Ten thousand miles away!'

I wish I were a bosun bold,
Or even a bombardier,
I'd build a boat and away I'd float,
And straight for my true love steer;
And straight for my true love steer, boys,
Where the dancing dolphins play,
And the whales and the sharks are having their larks
Ten thousand miles away.

The sun may shine through a London fog,
Or the river run quite clear;
The ocean's brine be turned to wine,
Or I forget my beer,
Or I forget my beer, my boys,
Or the landlord's quarter day,
Before I forget my own sweetheart
Ten thousand miles away.

Casey Jones

Come all you rounders if you want to hear
The story of a brave engineer;
Casey Jones was the hogger's name,
On a big eight-wheeler, boys, he won his fame.
Caller called Casey at half-past four;
He kissed his wife at the station door,
Mounted to the cabin with orders in his hand,
And took his farewell trip to the promised land.

Casey Jones, he mounted to the cabin,
Casey Jones, with his orders in his hand!
Casey Jones, he mounted to the cabin,
Took his farewell trip into the promised land.

'Put in your water and shovel in your coal,
Put your head out the window, watch the drivers roll.
I'll run her till she leaves the rail,
'Cause we're eight hours late with the Western Mail!'
He looked at his watch and his watch was slow,
Looked at the water and the water was low,
Turned to his fireboy and said,
'We'll get to 'Frisco, but we'll all be dead!'

Casey pulled up Reno Hill,
Tooted for the crossing with an awful shrill,
Snakes all knew by the engine's moans
That the hogger at the throttle was Casey Jones.
He pulled up short two miles from the place,
Number Four stared him right in the face;
Turned to his fireboy, said 'You'd better jump,
'Cause there's two locomotives that's going to bump!'

Casey said, just before he died,
'There's two more roads I'd like to ride.'
Fireboy said, 'What can they be?'
'The Rio Grande and the old S.P.'
Mrs. Jones sat on her bed a-sighing,
Got a pink* that Casey was dying,
Said, 'Go to bed, children; hush your crying,
'Cause you'll get another papa on the Salt Lake line.'

Casey Jones! Got another papa!
Casey Jones, on the Salt Lake line!
Casey Jones! Got another papa!
Got another papa on the Salt Lake line!

* a telegram

The ballad 'Durham Gaol', completed in 1852 was based on Tommy Armstrong's own experience, when he served a sentence in Durham Gaol for stealing a pair of stockings from the Co-op at West Stanley. He was drunk at the time and, from the way they were displayed, the stockings appeared to be bow-legged. Tommy was small and bow-legged and they seemed ideal for him.

Durham Gaol

You'll all have heard of Durham Gaol,
But it would you much surprise
To see the prisoners in the yard
When they're on exercise;
This yard is built around wi' walls
So noble and so strong:
Whoever goes there has to bide
His time, be it short or long.

   There's no good luck in Durham Gaol,
   There's no good luck at all;
   What is bread and skilly for,
   But just to make you small?

When you go to Durham Gaol,
They'll find you with employ;
They'll dress you up so dandy
In a suit o' corduroy.
They'll fetch a cap without a peak,
And never ask your size;
And like your suit it's corduroy
And comes down over your eyes.

The first month is the worst of all,
Your feelings they will try;
There's nowt but two great lumps o' wood
On which you have to lie.
Then after that you get to bed,
Well it's as hard as stones;
At night you dursn't make a turn,
For fear you break some bones.

All kinds o' work there going on
Upon these noble flats:
Teasin' oakum,* makin' balls,**
And weavin' coco mats.
When you go in you may be thin,
But they can make you thinner;
If your oakum is not teased,
They're sure to stop your dinner.

The shoes you get is often tens,
The smallest size is nine;
They're big enough to make a skiff

* unravelling lengths of rope and separating all the fibres
** probably a humorous reference to shot-drill, that is passing iron balls down a line of prisoners. During a quarter of an hour of this punishment a man would walk almost three kilometres, sideways, while picking up and putting down a 24-kg weight every three metres.

champion oarsman, at
a time when sculling on
the Tyne was a very
popular sport.

For Boyd*** upon the Tyne.
And if you should be cold at nights,
Just make yourself at home:
Wrap your clothes around your shoes
And get inside o' them.

You'll get your meat and clothes for nowt,
Your house and firin' free;
All your meat's brought to the door —
How happy you should be.
There's soap and towel, and wooden spoon,
And a little baby's pot;
They bring you papers every week
For you to clean your bot.

Tommy Armstrong

The Raggle Taggle Gypsies

'The Raggle Taggle Gypsies' is one of several versions of a Scottish ballad called 'The Gypsy Laddie'. It is also known as 'Black Jack Davy', 'The Dark-eyed Gypsie' and 'The Whistling Gypsy'.

The basic story in all these versions is of a newly-wed lady who leaves her wealth behind to go with the gypsies. The version which follows differs from 'The Gypsy Laddie' in that the lady leaves because she apparently prefers the life of the gypsies.

The Raggle Taggle Gypsies

Three gypsies stood at the castle gate,
They sang so high, they sang so low.
The lady sat in her chamber late,
Her heart it melted away as snow.

They sang so sweet, they sang so shrill,
That fast her tears began to flow.
And she laid down her silken gown,
Her golden rings and all her show.

She plucked off her high-heeled shoes,
A-made of Spanish leather, O.
She went in the street, with her bare, bare feet;
All out in the wind and weather, O.

Drawing by O. Soglow; © 1931, 1958
The New Yorker Magazine, Inc.

'O saddle to me my milk-white steed,
And go and fetch my pony, O
That I may ride and seek my bride,
Who is gone with the raggle taggle gypsies O.'

O he rode high and he rode low,
He rode through wood and copses too,
Until he came to an open field,
And there he espied his lady O.

'What makes you leave your house and land
Your golden treasures for to go
What makes you leave your new-wedded lord,
To follow the raggle taggle gypsies O.'

'What care I for my house and my land
What care I for my treasure O
What care I for my new-wedded lord,
I'm off with the raggle taggle gypsies O.'

'Last night you slept on a goose-feather bed,
With the sheets turned down so bravely O
And to-night you'll sleep in a cold open field,
Along with the raggle taggle gypsies O.'

'What care I for a goose-feather bed,
With the sheet turned down so bravely O
For to-night I shall sleep in a cold open field,
Along with the raggle taggle gypsies O.'

Group work

After your teacher has read 'The Raggle Taggle Gypsies' aloud
to the whole class, organise a reading within your group. We
suggest that two of you read the parts that are narrated, with
one person reading the dialogue of the 'new-wedded lord' and
another person that of the lady.

When your group has read the poem aloud, talk about it in
order to understand the story more clearly. Make some notes
for yourselves, on the events that the ballad relates.

The following notes show some of the ways in which this
poem can be considered a typical ballad:

A ballad is a song which tells a story. Traditional ballads were not written down but were passed on from the original composer by word of mouth. Other ballad singers often altered the words, either to suit themselves or because they forgot some of the details of the version they first heard. In this way too, ballads changed as they passed from one generation to another.

'The Raggle Taggle Gypsies' was popular as far afield as Scotland, Devon, Ireland and America, and as it would have travelled by word of mouth, it is hardly surprising that very different versions were sung in each of these areas.

As with many ballads, much of the action of 'The Raggle Taggle Gypsies' is carried forward by dialogue. In other words, we learn much of the story through what the characters say.

Ballads concentrate on the action of the story. They use a technique which is similar to that used in plays or films, and only describe a series of important scenes or the most important event in the story.

As a group, discuss the way in which:

dialogue helps to tell the story,

the story is told in three short scenes.

Exploring the ballad

Group work

This section is designed to introduce you to four ballads: 'Lord Randal', 'Botany Bay', 'The Cruel War' and 'The Ballad of Birmingham'. In your present groups (**working groups**) you will be working on one of these ballads in detail. Then your teacher will help you to form new groups (**sharing groups**) with three new people from different working groups. In your sharing groups you will be teaching the other three students about your ballad, and they will explain their ballads to you.

Your teacher will help you to select the ballads for your working group.

Working groups

1. Read your ballad through silently first. Then read it aloud within your group. You may decide to choose some of the group to read the narration and others to read the dialogue.

2. Talk about the ballad and make some notes outlining the story. If you have any problems, ask your teacher.

3. In your sharing groups you will be together with one person from each of three other groups who have looked at other ballads. The following preparation is designed to help you to share your enjoyment of your ballad with them.

- Write a short introduction to prepare the others in your sharing group for the reading of your ballad. Give them some information about the ballad that will make it easier for them to follow.

- Practise reading your ballad aloud by yourself.

- Imagine that you have heard of the events related in your ballad. In your own words, tell the story of the incident. Practise telling this to others in your group.

- Discuss how dialogue advances the plot – that is, moves the story along.

- Discuss the way in which your ballad tells its story.

4. Check your understanding of the last two ideas with your teacher to make sure that they are clear in your mind.

Suggestions for sharing groups

Here is one way to share what has happened so far:

- The student whose group has looked at 'Lord Randal' would give a short introduction, read the ballad and tell the story in his or her own words.

- The group should then compare the way dialogue is used in each of the four ballads and prepare a short statement for the rest of the class. Be prepared to discuss this with your teacher.

- Discuss how you would go about making your ballads into short plays. Are they all suitable? Prepare a statement for the rest of the class.

- Your teacher will organise a short, whole-class discussion.

Lord Randal

Oh, where have you been, Lord Randal, my son?
Oh, where have you been, my handsome young man? –
Oh, I've been to the wildwood; mother, make my bed soon,
I'm weary of hunting and I fain would lie down.

And whom did you meet there, Lord Randal, my son?
And whom did you meet there, my handsome young man? –
Oh, I met with my true love; mother, make my bed soon,
I'm weary of hunting and I fain would lie down.

What got you for supper, Lord Randal, my son?
What got you for supper, my handsome young man? –
I got eels boiled in broth; mother, make my bed soon,
I'm weary of hunting and I fain would lie down.

And who got your leavings, Lord Randal, my son?
And who got your leavings, my handsome young man? –
I gave them to my dogs; mother, make my bed soon,
I'm weary of hunting and I fain would lie down.

And what did your dogs do, Lord Randal, my son?
And what did your dogs do, my handsome young man? –
Oh, they stretched out and died; mother, make my bed soon,
I'm weary of hunting and I fain would lie down.

Oh, I fear you are poisoned, Lord Randal, my son,
Oh, I fear you are poisoned, my handsome young man? –
Oh, yes, I am poisoned; mother, make my bed soon,
I'm weary of hunting and I fain would lie down.

What will you leave your mother, Lord Randal, my son?
What will you leave your mother, my handsome young man? –
My house and my lands; mother, make my bed soon,
I'm weary of hunting and I fain would lie down.

What will you leave your sister, Lord Randal, my son?
What will you leave your sister, my handsome young man? –
My gold and my silver; mother, make my bed soon,
I'm weary of hunting and I fain would lie down.

What will you leave your brother, Lord Randal, my son?
What will you leave your brother, my handsome young man? –
My horse and my saddle; mother, make my bed soon,
I'm weary of hunting and I fain would lie down.

What will you leave your true-love, Lord Randal, my son?
What will you leave your true-love, my handsome young man? –
A halter to hang her; mother, make my bed soon,
For I'm sick at the heart and I want to lie down.

Botany Bay

Come all young men of learning and a warning take by me,
I would have you quit night walking and shun bad company;
I would have you quit night walking, or else you'll rue the day,
You'll rue your transporation, lads, when you're bound for
    Botany Bay.

I was brought up in London Town at a place I know full well,
Brought up by honest parents, for the truth to you I'll tell;
Brought up by honest parents and reared most tenderly,
Till I became a roving blade, which proved my destiny.

My character soon was taken and I was sent to jail;
My friends they tried to clear me but nothing could prevail.
At the Old Bailey Sessions the judge to me did say,
'The jury's found you guilty lad, you must go to Botany Bay.'

To see my agèd father dear as he stood at the bar,
Likewise my tender mother, her old grey locks to tear;
In tearing of her old grey locks, these words to me did say,
'Oh son, oh son, what have you done, that you're going to
    Botany Bay?'

It was on the twenty-eighth of May, from England we did steer;
And all things being made safe on board we sailed down the
    river clear;
And every ship that we passed by, we heard the sailors say,
'There goes a ship of clever hands, and they're bound for
    Botany Bay.'

There is a girl in Manchester, a girl I know full well;
And if ever I get my liberty, along with her I'll dwell.
Oh, then I mean to marry her and no more go astray;
I'll shun all evil company, bid adieu to Botany Bay.

The Cruel War

A ballad from the American Civil War, 1861–5

The cruel war is raging and Johnny has to fight,
I want to be with him from morning till night.
I want to be with him, it grieves my heart so,
Oh, let me go with you; no my love, no.

I'd go to your captain, get down on my knees,
Ten thousand gold guineas I would give for your release;
Ten thousand gold guineas, it grieves my heart so,
Won't you let me go with you? – no, my love, no.

Tomorrow is Sunday and Monday is the day
Your captain calls for you and you must obey;
Your captain calls for you, it grieves my heart so,
Won't you let me go with you? – no, my love, no.

Your waist is too slender, your fingers are too small,
Your cheeks are too rosy to face the cannon ball;
Your cheeks are too rosy, it grieves my heart so,
Won't you let me go with you? – no, my love, no.

I'll tie back my hair, men's clothing I'll put on;
I'll pass for your comrade as we march along;
I'll pass as your comrade, no one will ever know,
Won't you let me go with you? – no, my love, no.

Johnny, oh Johnny, I think you are unkind,
I love you far better than all other mankind;
I love you far better than words can e'er express,
Won't you let me go with you? – yes, my love, yes.

Ballad of Birmingham

'Mother dear, may I go downtown
instead of out to play,
and march the streets of Birmingham
in a freedom march today?'

'No, baby, no, you may not go,
for the dogs are fierce and wild,
and clubs and hoses, guns and jails
ain't good for a little child.'

'But, mother, I won't be alone.
Other children will go with me,
and march the streets of Birmingham
to make our country free.'

'No, baby, no, you may not go,
for I fear those guns will fire.
But you may go to church instead,
and sing in the children's choir.'

She has combed and brushed her nightdark hair,
and bathed rose petal sweet,
and drawn white gloves on her small brown hands,
and white shoes on her feet.

The mother smiled to know her child
was in the sacred place,
but that smile was the last smile
to come upon her face.

For when she heard the explosion,
her eyes grew wet and wild.
She raced through the streets of Birmingham
calling for her child.

She clawed through bits of glass and brick,
then lifted out a shoe.
'O, here's the shoe my baby wore,
but, baby, where are you?'

Dudley Randall

The ballad as poetry

The emphasis so far in this chapter has been placed on ballads as stories. In many cases these ballads have only survived for hundreds of years because of their qualities as poems and songs.

These are some of the characteristics of ballads as poetry:

- The poem's rhythm is important in establishing the mood of the ballad.
- Most ballads are broken up into four-line stanzas.
- Rhyme is an important feature of most ballads.
- Repetition is used a great deal.
- Many ballads have a chorus or refrain which is repeated after each stanza.

All these characteristics have made, and still make, ballads easier to remember. Today's pop songs use many of these techniques for the same reason.

1. Focus on any ballad in this chapter and discuss these characteristics. To what extent are these characteristics present in that ballad? Show your teacher that you understand what **rhythm**, **rhyme**, **stanza**, **repetition** and **chorus** all mean. Also show that you understand how they've been used in your ballad.

2. In your small group examine several ballads from the chapter in order to answer the following questions. Before you start, arrange to get together with another group that has looked at the same ballads as you so that you can compare your answers.

- Compare the rhythm of the various ballads. How does the rhythm reflect the mood of the ballad? For example, you might expect that a ballad which tells a sad story would be told in a slow, mournful rhythm.

- Compare the use of rhyme in the ballads you've chosen. In which ballad do you think rhyme has been used most effectively? Why?

- Compare the use of repetition in your ballads. Is it more effective in some than in others? Explain your answer.

3. Join together with the other group and share your answers to these questions.

4. Your teacher may decide to have a whole class discussion so that some ideas may be shared more widely.

Writing a ballad

A possible approach

1. Make a list of the topics that all the ballads in this chapter deal with. What kinds of topics seem most popular?

2. In your groups, discuss the statement that 'the stories which in the past were narrated in ballad form are now told on television.' Would these ballads make good television drama?

3. *Selecting a topic for your own ballad*

    Either

    (a) Write a ballad about a television series, a film, a novel or short story that you have enjoyed.

    or

    (b) Choose an event of topical interest, or a person who has recently been in the news, to write your ballad about.

4. *Writing the ballad*

    Make some notes for yourself on the story you wish to tell.

    Work out the major events or scenes that you will describe. Try to keep these to as few as possible – three might be a good number.

    Can you use dialogue in telling your story?

    For your first attempt you might want to use the tune of a well-known ballad. If not, what rhythm will suit your story? As you write you'll need to be conscious of this. If necessary look at the ballads in this chapter for help.

    Will you use four-line stanzas?

    How will you organise your rhyme scheme? Using rhyme for the second and fourth lines of each stanza may be the easiest way.

    Can you use repetition? A chorus?

5. You need to write the first draft of your ballad and then work on improving the quality of the rhyme and rhythm. For almost every word you'll need to ask the following questions:

    Is it the best word to use?

    Is it necessary?

    Does it say exactly what I want to say?

6. Work with the other members of your group in revising your draft (or drafts) and ask them to help you improve your ballad. Ask your teacher for help if you need to.

7. When you are satisfied with your work, ask your group to help read your ballad to the whole class.

Towards a class concert

This chapter on ballads lends itself to the presentation of a class concert. If your teacher decides to take up this idea, each group could present a piece of drama and either some singing or choral speaking. A suitable finale to such a concert could be the whole class singing a ballad.

Drama

As a group of four, organise an improvised version of your ballad. Make it a serious attempt to explain the story. Try to make each of the characters clear to your audience. It is important in an improvised version to avoid following the dialogue of the ballad too closely.

Discuss how you'll treat the story. When you've worked out your sketch, rehearse it a few times and be prepared to present it at the class concert.

Choral speaking or singing

Decide which ballad you wish to present at the concert. It may be the one you have studied, another from this chapter or a ballad with which you are familiar.

You may wish to join forces with other students to form a larger group to sing at the concert. It should be possible to find someone to accompany you on either piano or guitar.

Whether you are speaking or singing, decide how you'll present the ballad and who'll take which parts. Practise. You may even decide to memorise the ballad for your presentation.

Reflection

Discuss these questions in your journal, or in your groups:

- Which of the ballads have you enjoyed the most? Why?

- What do you think is the most important thing you've learned in this chapter?

- What have you enjoyed most? Explain your answer.

If anything you have studied in this chapter has made you curious to know more, or if the chapter has suggested interesting fields of study, talk to your teacher about this.

Further reading

Penguin Book of Ballads
Oxford Book of Ballads
Faber Book of Ballads

Ballads

British:	The Robin Hood ballads
	'Sir Patrick Spens'
	'The Douglas Tragedy'
	'The Cherry-Tree Carol'
	'Edward, Edward'
	'The Three Ravens'
	'The Unquiet Grave'
	'Barbara Allen'
	'Helen of Kirkconnell'
American:	'Frankie and Johnny'
	'Tom Dooley'
	'John Henry'
	'The Boll Weevil'
	'Jesse James'
	'The Streets of Laredo'
Australian:	'The Banks of the Condamine'
	'Moreton Bay'
	'South Australia'
	'The Dying Stockman'
	'The Old Bark Hut'
	'The Overlanders'
	'Flash Jack from Gundagai'
	'The Wild Colonial Boy'

7 Folk tales

Here are two English folk tales that have come down to us through hundreds of years. You will probably notice something interesting about these two stories.

They are best read aloud and your teacher is likely to begin this chapter by reading the stories to the whole class. You can then read them over silently to yourself to see if they remind you of any other story that you know.

Tattercoats

In a great palace by the sea there once dwelt a very rich old lord, who had neither wife nor children living, only one little grand-daughter, whose face he had never seen in all her life. He hated her bitterly, because at her birth his favourite daughter died; and when the old nurse brought him the baby, he swore, that it might live or die as it liked, but he would never look on its face as long as it lived.

So he turned his back, and sat by his window looking out over the sea, and weeping great tears for his lost daughter, till his white hair and beard grew down over his shoulders and twined round his chair and crept into the chinks of the floor, and his tears, dropping on to the window-ledge, wore a channel through the stone, and ran away in a little river to the great sea. And, meanwhile, his granddaughter grew up with no one to care for her, or clothe her; only the old nurse, when no one was by, would sometimes give her a dish of scraps from the kitchen, or a torn petticoat from the rag-bag; while the other servants of the palace would drive her from the house with blows and mocking words, calling her 'Tattercoats', and pointing at her bare feet and shoulders, till she ran away crying, to hide among the bushes.

And so she grew up, with little to eat or wear, spending her days in the fields and lanes, with only the gooseherd for a companion, who would play to her so merrily on his little pipe, when she was hungry, or cold, or tired, that she forgot all her troubles, and fell to dancing, with his flock of noisy geese for partners.

But, one day, people told each other that the king was travelling through the land, and in the town near by was to give a great ball, to all the lords and ladies of the country, when the prince, his only son, was to choose a wife.

One of the royal invitations was brought to the palace by the sea, and the servants carried it up to the old lord, who still sat by his window, wrapped in his long white hair and weeping into the little river that was fed by his tears.

But when he heard the king's command, he dried his eyes and bade them bring shears to cut him loose, for his hair had bound him a fast prisoner and he could not move. And then he sent them for rich clothes, and jewels, which he put on; and he ordered them to saddle the white horse, with gold and silk, that he might ride to meet the king.

Meanwhile Tattercoats had heard of the great doings in the town, and she sat by the kitchen-door weeping because she could not go to see them. And when the old nurse heard her crying she went to the lord of the palace, and begged him to take his grand-daughter with him to the king's ball.

But he only frowned and told her to be silent, while the servants laughed and said: 'Tattercoats is happy in her rags, playing with the gooseherd, let her be – it is all she is fit for.'

A second, and then a third time, the old nurse begged him to let the girl go with him, but she was answered only by black looks and fierce words, till she was driven from the room by the jeering servants, with blows and mocking words.

Weeping over her ill success, the old nurse went to look for Tattercoats; but the girl had been turned from the door by the cook, and had run away to tell her friend the gooseherd how unhappy she was because she could not go to the king's ball.

But when the gooseherd had listened to her story, he bade her cheer up, and proposed that they should go together into the town to see the king, and all the fine things; and when she looked sorrowfully down at her rags and bare feet, he played a note or two upon his pipe, so gay and merry that she forgot all about her tears, and her troubles, and before she well knew, the herdboy had taken her by the hand, and she, and he, and the geese before them, were dancing down the road towards the town.

Before they had gone very far, a handsome young man, splendidly dressed, rode up and stopped to ask the way to the castle where the king was staying; and when he found that they, too, were going thither, he got off his horse and walked beside them along the road.

The herdboy pulled out his pipe and played a low sweet tune, and the stranger looked again and again at Tattercoats' lovely face till he fell deeply in love with her, and begged her to marry him.

But she only laughed, and shook her golden head. 'You would be finely put to shame if you had a goosegirl for your wife!' said she; 'go and ask one of the great ladies you will see tonight at the king's ball, and do not flout poor Tattercoats.'

But the more she refused him the sweeter the pipe played, and the deeper the young man fell in love; till at last he begged her, as a proof of his sincerity, to come that night at twelve to the king's ball, just as she was, with the herdboy and his geese, and in her torn petticoat and bare feet, and he would dance with her before the king and the lords and ladies, and present her to them all, as his dear and honoured bride.

So when night came, and the hall in the castle was full of light and music, and the lords and ladies were dancing before the king, just as the clock struck twelve, Tattercoats and the herdboy, followed by his flock of noisy geese, entered at the great doors, and walked straight up the ballroom, while on either side the ladies whispered, the lords laughed, and the king seated at the far end stared in amazement.

But as they came in front of the throne, Tattercoats' lover rose from beside the king, and came to meet her. Taking her by the hand, he kissed her thrice before them all, and turned to the king.

'Father!' he said, for it was the prince himself, 'I have made my choice, and here is my bride, the loveliest girl in all the land, and the sweetest as well!'

Before he had finished speaking, the herdboy put his pipe to his lips and played a few low notes that sounded like a bird singing far off in the woods; and as he played, Tattercoats' rags were changed to shining robes sewn with glittering jewels, a golden crown lay upon her golden hair, and the flock of geese behind her became a crowd of dainty pages, bearing her long train.

And as the king rose to greet her as his daughter, the trumpets sounded loudly in honour of the new princess, and the people outside in the street said to each other:

'Ah! now the prince has chosen for his wife the loveliest girl in all the land!'

But the gooseherd was never seen again, and no one knew what became of him; while the old lord went home once more to his palace by the sea, for he could not stay at court, when he had sworn never to look on his granddaughter's face.

So there he still sits by his window, if you could only see him, as you some day may, weeping more bitterly than ever, as he looks out over the sea.

Cap o' Rushes

Well, there was once a very rich gentleman, and he had three daughters, and he thought he'd see how fond they were of him. So he says to the first, 'How much do you love me, my dear?'

'Why,' says she, 'as I love my life.'

'That's good,' says he.

So he says to the second, 'How much do *you* love me, my dear?'

'Why,' says she, 'better nor all the world.'

'That's good,' says he.

So he says to the third, 'How much do *you* love me, my dear?'

'Why, I love you as fresh meat loves salt,' says she.

Well, but he was angry. 'You don't love me at all,' says he, 'and in my house you stay no more.' So he drove her out there and then, and shut the door in her face.

Well, she went away on and on till she came to a fen, and there she gathered a lot of rushes and made them into a kind of a sort of a cloak with a hood, to cover her from head to foot, and to hide her fine clothes. And then she went on and on till she came to a great house.

'Do you want a maid?' says she.

'No, we don't,' said they.

'I haven't nowhere to go,' says she; 'and I ask no wages, and do any sort of work,' says she.

'Well,' said they, 'if you like to wash the pots and scrape the saucepans you may stay,' said they.

So she stayed there and washed the pots and scraped the saucepans and did all the dirty work. And because she gave no name they called her 'Cap o' Rushes'.

Well, one day there was to be a great dance a little way off, and the servants were allowed to go and look on at the grand people. Cap o' Rushes said she was too tired to go, so she stayed at home.

But when they were gone, she offed with her cap o' rushes, and cleaned herself, and went to the dance. And no one there was so finely dressed as she.

Well, who should be there but her master's son, and what should he do but fall in love with her the minute he set eyes on her. He wouldn't dance with anyone else.

But before the dance was done, Cap o' Rushes slipped off, and away she went home. And when the other maids came back, she was pretending to be asleep with her cap o' rushes on.

Well, next morning they said to her, 'You did miss a sight, Cap o' Rushes!'

'What was that?' says she.

'Why, the beautifullest lady you ever did see, dressed right gay and ga'. The young master, he never took his eyes off her.'

'Well, I should have liked to have seen her,' says Cap o' Rushes.

'Well, there's to be another dance this evening, and perhaps she'll be there.'

But, come the evening, Cap o' Rushes said she was too tired to go with them. Howsoever, when they were gone, she offed with her cap o' rushes and cleaned herself, and away she went to the dance.

The master's son had been reckoning on seeing her, and he danced with no one else, and never took his eyes off her. But, before the dance was over, she slipped off, and home she went, and when the maids came back she pretended to be asleep with her cap o' rushes on.

Next day they said to her again, 'Well, Cap o' Rushes, you should ha' been there to see the lady. There she was again, gay and ga', and the young master he never took his eyes off her.'

'Well, there,' says she, 'I should ha' liked to ha' seen her.'

'Well,' says they, 'there's a dance again this evening, and you must go with us, for she's sure to be there.'

Well, come this evening, Cap o' Rushes said she was too tired to go, and do what they would she stayed at home. But when they were gone, she offed her cap o' rushes and cleaned herself, and away she went to the dance.

The master's son was rarely glad when he saw her. He danced with none but her and never took his eyes off her. When she wouldn't tell him her name, nor where she came from, he gave her a ring and told her if he didn't see her again he should die.

Well, before the dance was over, off she slipped, and home she went, and when the maids came home she was pretending to be asleep with her cap o' rushes on.

Well, next day they says to her, 'There, Cap o' Rushes, you didn't come last night, and now you won't see the lady, for there's no more dances.'

'Well, I should have rarely liked to have seen her,' says she.

The master's son tried every way to find out where the lady was gone, but go where he might, and ask whom he might he never heard anything about her. And he got worse and worse for the love of her till he had to keep to his bed.

'Make some gruel for the young master,' they said to the cook. 'He's dying for the love of the lady.' The cook set about making it when Cap o' Rushes came in.

'What are you a-doing of?' says she.

'I'm going to make some gruel for the young master,' says the cook, 'for he's dying for love of the lady.'

'Let me make it,' says Cap o' Rushes.

Well, the cook wouldn't at first, but at last she said yes, and Cap o' Rushes made the gruel. And when she had made it, she slipped the ring into it on the sly before the cook took it upstairs.

The young man he drank it and then he saw the ring at the bottom.

'Send for the cook,' says he.

So up she comes.

'Who made this gruel here?' says he.

'I did,' says the cook, for she was frightened.

And he looked at her.

'No, you didn't,' says he. 'Say who did, and you shan't be harmed.'

'Well, then, t'was Cap o' Rushes,' says she.

'Send Cap o' Rushes here,' says he.

So Cap o' Rushes came.

'Did you make my gruel?' says he.

'Yes, I did,' says she.

'Where did you get this ring?' says he.

'From him that gave it me,' says she.

'Who are you, then?' says the young man.

'I'll show you,' says she. And she offed with her cap o' rushes, and there she was in her beautiful clothes.

Well, the master's son he got well very soon, and they were to be married in a little time. It was to be a very grand wedding, and everyone was asked far and near. And Cap o' Rushes' father was asked. But she never told anybody who she was.

But before the wedding, she went to the cook, and says she:

'I want you to dress every dish without a mite o' salt.'

'That'll be rare nasty,' says the cook.

'That doesn't signify,' says she.

'Very well,' says the cook.

Well, the wedding day came, and they were married. And after they were married, all the company sat down to the dinner. When they began to eat the meat, it was so tasteless they couldn't eat it. But Cap o' Rushes's father tried first one dish and then another, and then he burst out crying.

'What is the matter?' said the master's son to him.

'Oh!' says he, 'I had a daughter. And I asked her how much she loved me. And she said "As much as fresh meat loves salt." And I turned her from my door, for I thought she didn't love me. And now I see she loved me best of all. And she may be dead for aught I know.'

'No, father, here she is!' said Cap o' Rushes. And she goes up to him and puts her arms round him.

And so they were all happy ever after.

Group work

1. In your groups, discuss the two stories you have just read, and make up a group list of the similarities and the differences you can see between them. You might like to consider the similarities and differences between:

	Similarities	Differences
plot		
characters		
dialogue		
setting		
ending		

Start at the beginning of each story, and work your way through carefully, comparing the two and making your list as you go. It might be helpful if two people in the group look at 'Tattercoats', and two look at 'Cap o' Rushes'.

2. When you have completed your list, and you're satisfied that you have as much evidence as you can find, try to come to a conclusion about these stories, by weighing up the two lists of evidence you've compiled.

Are they different versions of the same story?

or

Are they two different stories altogether?

3. Share your conclusions with the whole class, explaining the reasons for your deductions, to see whether other groups came to the same conclusions as you did.

Individual work

Now here is a third story, 'Rushen Coatie'. Read this through to yourself, and look for any clues that suggest it is either another version of the first two stories, or a completely different story altogether.

Rushen Coatie

There was once a king and a queen, as many a one has been; few have we seen, and as few may we see. But the queen died, leaving only one bonny girl, and she told her on her deathbed: 'My dear, after I am gone, there will come to you a little red calf, and whenever you want anything, speak to it, and it will give it you.'

Now, after a while, the king married again an ill-natured wife with three ugly daughters of her own. And they hated the king's daughter because she was so bonny. So they took all her fine clothes away from her, and gave her only a coat made of rushes. So they called her Rushen Coatie, and made her sit in the kitchen nook, amid the ashes. And when dinner-time came, the nasty stepmother sent her out a thimbleful of broth, a grain of barley, a thread of meat, and a crumb of bread. But when she had eaten all this, she was just as hungry as before, so she said to herself: 'Oh! how I wish I had something to eat.' Just then, who should come in but a little red calf, and said to her: 'Put your finger into my left ear.' She did so, and found some nice bread. Then the calf told her to put her finger into its right ear, and she found there some cheese, and made a right good meal of the bread and cheese. And so it went on from day to day.

Now the king's wife thought Rushen Coatie would soon die from the scanty food she got, and she was surprised to see her as lively and healthy as ever. So she set one of her ugly daughters on the watch at meal-times to find out how Rushen Coatie got enough to live on. The daughter soon found out that the red calf gave food to Rushen Coatie, and told her mother. So her mother went to the king and told him she was longing to have a sweet-bread from a red calf. Then the king sent for his butcher, and had the little calf killed. And when Rushen Coatie heard of it, she sat down and wept by its side, but the dead calf said:

'Take me up, bone by bone,
And put me beneath yon grey stone;
When there is aught you want
Tell it me, and that I'll grant.'

So she did so, but could not find the shank-bone of the calf.

Now the very next Sunday was Yuletide, and all the folk were going to church in their best clothes, so Rushen Coatie said: 'Oh! I should like to go to church, too', but the three ugly sisters said: 'What would you do at the church, you nasty thing? You must bide at home and make the dinner.' And the king's wife said: 'And this is what you must make the soup of, a thimbleful of water, a grain of barley, and a crumb of bread.'

When they all went to church, Rushen Coatie sat down and wept, but looking up, who should she see coming in limping, lamping, with a shank wanting, but the dear red calf? And the red calf said to her: 'Do not sit there weeping, but go, put on these clothes, and above all, put on this pair of glass slippers, and go your way to church.'

'But what will become of the dinner?' said Rushen Coatie.

'Oh, do not fash about that,' said the red calf; 'all you have to do is to say to the fire:

'"Every peat make t'other burn,
Every spit make t'other turn,
Every pot make t'other play,
Till I come from church this good Yuleday,"

and be off to church with you. But mind you come home first.'

So Rushen Coatie said this, and went off to church, and she was the grandest and finest lady there. There happened to be a young prince there, and he fell at once in love with her. But she came away before service was over, and was home before the rest, and had off with her fine clothes and on with her rushen coatie, and she found the calf had covered the table, and the dinner was ready, and everything was in good order when the rest came home. The three sisters said to Rushen Coatie: 'Eh, lassie, if you had seen the bonny fine lady in church today, that the young prince fell in love with!' Then she said: 'Oh! I wish you would let me go with you to the church tomorrow', for they used to go three days together to church at Yuletide.

But they said: 'What should the like of you do at church, nasty thing? The kitchen nook is good enough for you.'

So the next day they all went to church, and Rushen Coatie was left behind, to make dinner out of a thimbleful of water, a grain of barley, a crumb of bread, and a thread of meat. But the red calf came to her help again, gave her finer clothes than before, and she went to church, where all the world was looking at her, and wondering where such a grand lady came from, and the prince fell more in love with her than ever, and tried to find out where she went to. But she was too quick for him, and got home long before the rest, and the red calf had the dinner all ready.

The next day the calf dressed her in even grander clothes than before, and she went to the church. And the young prince was there again, and this time he put a guard at the door to keep her, but she took a hop and a run and jumped over their heads, and as she did so, down fell one of her glass slippers. She didn't wait to pick it up, you may be sure, but off she ran home, as fast as she could go, on with the rushen coatie, and the calf had all things ready.

The young prince put out a proclamation that whoever could put on the glass slipper should be his bride. All the ladies of his court went and tried to put on the slipper. And they tried and tried and tried, but it was too small for them all. Then he ordered one of his ambassadors to mount a fleet horse and ride through the kingdom and find an owner for the glass shoe. He rode and he rode to town and castle, and made all the ladies try to put on the shoe. Many a one tried to get it on that she might be the prince's bride. But no, it wouldn't do, and many a one wept, I warrant, because she couldn't get on the bonny glass shoe. The ambassador rode on, and on till he came at the very last to the house where there were the three ugly sisters. The first two tried it and it wouldn't do, and the queen, mad with spite, hacked off the toes and heels of the third sister, and she could then put the slipper on, and the prince was brought to marry her, for he had to keep his promise. The ugly sister was dressed all in her best and was put up behind the prince on horseback, and off they rode in great gallantry. But ye all know, pride must have a fall, for as they rode along a raven sang out of a bush –

> 'Hackèd Heels and Pinchèd Toes
> Behind the young prince rides,
> But Pretty Feet and Little Feet
> Behind the cauldron bides.'

'What's that the birdie sings?' said the young prince.

'Nasty, lying thing,' said the stepsister, 'never mind what it says.'

But the prince looked down and saw the slipper dripping with blood, so he rode back and put her down. Then he said, 'There must be someone that the slipper has not been tried on.'

'Oh, no,' said they, 'there's none but a dirty thing that sits in the kitchen nook and wears a rushen coatie.'

But the prince was determined to try it on Rushen Coatie, but she ran away to the grey stone, where the red calf dressed her in her bravest dress, and she went to the prince and the slipper jumped out of his pocket on to her foot, fitting her without any chipping or paring. So the prince married her that very day, and they lived happy ever after.

When you have had time to think about 'Rushen Coatie' in comparison with the first two stories, share your thoughts with the people in your group to see if you came to the same conclusions.

If you agree with each other, move on to the next section. If you don't agree with each other, make sure that you can understand all the opinions before you move on.

Whole class work

1. Have a look at home, in the school library, in the local library, or ask other people around school, so that you can collect as many versions of the fairy story, 'Cinderella', as you can. Pass these around the class, or ask your teacher, or some volunteers, to read a couple of versions aloud to you.

2.

WHAT DO YOU THINK?

You may now have heard, seen, read and collected enough evidence to examine the theory:

'Cinderella' is not original.

Do you agree?

(a) Spend five or ten minutes in a whole-class brainstorming session, presenting arguments **for** and **against** the theory. Your teacher might list your ideas on the blackboard as you go, using two columns – one for each side of the argument.

(b) When all the ideas are listed on the board, discuss each of them in your group, and select the **best** argument for each side.

(c) Groups can now share the points they have selected with the rest of the class. Discuss the arguments that the groups have **rejected** to clarify why they were not as good.

Individual and pairs work

1. Prepare a written argument for your teacher, examining the theory: **'Cinderella' is not original**
from one side only. Use evidence collected from your own detective work, and from what you heard in the class discussion.

2. Prepare and perform an interview in pairs, one person stating one side of the argument while the other person tries to change their mind,

   or

   Write this argument in pairs, taking it in turns to respond to what the other person has said.

3. Choose any one of the stories you have read in this chapter, and turn it into a play for the rest of the class. You can use your imagination about time and setting.

4. Try turning one of these stories into a ballad, telling the story in verse. You might even want to set your ballad to music if you know a tune that would suit.

5. Can you think of any other stories you have read where the **idea** or **theme** of the Cinderella story is used? The idea of 'rags to riches' is used by many authors, even today.

   Try writing your own 'rags to riches' story, either as a modern-day version of the Cinderella tale, or inventing your own version.

6. Many cultures have their own versions of the Cinderella story. If you know anyone from Vietnam, India or the Middle Eastern countries, ask them if they can discover a version of Cinderella from their homeland. Share these stories with the rest of the class.

Reflection

The work in this chapter has involved your examining these folk tales very carefully, in order to find similarities and differences between them.

Did you find that the 'detective' work you did proved helpful when you came to write your own arguments, interviews, plays, ballads or stories? Discuss this in your group before sharing your ideas in a whole class discussion.

Most people have heard of 'Cinderella' as one of many children's fairy tales. Talk in your group about other fairy tales that you remember from your own childhood. Then spend some time writing in your journal about your own favourite childhood stories, and why you liked them.

8 Examining a theme: the cost of progress

This chapter gives you the opportunity to examine the advantages and disadvantages that come with 'progress'. It will also give you the opportunity to learn some of the skills of successful argument.

You will find a short story, 'The Flying Machine', by Ray Bradbury, an essay, 'It's the Letrit!' by 'Cassandra', and a song 'Where do the Children Play?' by Cat Stevens, to use as a starting point for your argument. Each piece challenges us to think carefully about progress.

Something to think about:

> TECHNOLOGY IS TERRIFIC

● Do you agree?

● Check your dictionary for the double meaning of 'terrific' before deciding.

● What do the others in your group think?

For the teacher
You might begin this unit by reading 'The Flying Machine' aloud to the class. Useful additional resources for this unit include:

● a recording of 'Where Do the Children Play?' from Cat Stevens; *Tea for the Tillerman* (Island) or *Cat Stevens' Greatest Hits Volume 2* (Island).

● film *The Flying Machine*, U.S., 1979, 16 minutes, colour, Director – Bernard Selling, Glanbuck Films.

The Flying Machine
by *Ray Bradbury*

In the year AD 400, the Emperor Yuan held his throne by the Great Wall of China, and the land was green with rain, readying itself toward the harvest, at peace, the people in his dominion neither too happy nor too sad.

Early on the morning of the first day of the first week of the second month of the new year, the Emperor Yuan was sipping tea and fanning himself against a warm breeze when a servant ran across the scarlet and blue garden tiles, calling, 'Oh, Emperor, Emperor, a miracle!'

'Yes,' said the Emperor, 'the air is sweet this morning.'

'No, no, a miracle!' said the servant, bowing quickly.

'And this tea is good in my mouth, surely that is a miracle.'

'No, no, Your Excellency.'

'Let me guess then – the sun has risen and a new day is upon us. Or the sea is blue. That now is the finest of all miracles.'

'Excellency, a man is flying!'

'What?' The Emperor stopped his fan.

'I saw him in the air, a man flying with wings. I heard a voice call out of the sky, and when I looked up, there he was, a dragon in the heavens with a man in its mouth, a dragon of paper and bamboo, coloured like the sun and the grass.'

'It is early,' said the Emperor, 'and you have just wakened from a dream.'

'It is early, but I have seen what I have seen! Come, and you will see it too.'

'Sit down with me here,' said the Emperor. 'Drink some tea. It must be a strange thing, if it is true, to see a man fly. You must have time to think of it, even as I must have time to prepare myself for the sight.'

They drank tea.

'Please,' said the servant at last, 'or he will be gone.'

The Emperor rose thoughtfully. 'Now you may show me what you have seen.'

They walked into a garden, across a meadow of grass, over a small bridge, through a grove of trees, and up a tiny hill.

'There!' said the servant.

The Emperor looked into the sky.

And in the sky, laughing so high that you could hardly hear him laugh, was a man; and the man was clothed in bright papers and reeds to make wings and a beautiful yellow tail, and he was soaring all about like the largest bird in a universe of birds, like a new dragon in a land of ancient dragons.

The man called down to them from high in the cool winds of morning, 'I fly, I fly!'

The servant waved to him. 'Yes, yes!'

The Emperor Yuan did not move. Instead he looked at the Great Wall of China now taking shape out of the farthest mist in the green hills, that splendid snake of stones which writhed with majesty across the entire land. That wonderful wall which had protected them for a timeless time from enemy hordes and preserved peace for years without number. He saw the town nestled to itself by a river and a road and a hill, beginning to waken.

'Tell me,' he said to his servant, 'has anyone else seen this flying man?'

'I am the only one, Excellency,' said the servant, smiling at the sky, waving.

The Emperor watched the heavens another minute and then said, 'Call him down to me.'

'Ho, come down, come down! The Emperor wishes to see you!' called the servant, hands cupped to his shouting mouth.

The Emperor glanced in all directions while the flying man soared down the morning wind. He saw a farmer, early in his fields, watching the sky, and he noted where the farmer stood. The flying man alit with a rustle of paper and a creak of bamboo reeds. He came proudly to the Emperor, clumsy in his rig, at last bowing before the old man.

'What have you done?' demanded the Emperor.

'I have flown in the sky, Your Excellency,' replied the man.

'What have you done?' said the Emperor again.

'I have just told you!' cried the flier.

'You have told me nothing at all.' The Emperor reached out a thin hand to touch the pretty paper and the birdlike keel of the apparatus. It smelled cool, of the wind.

'Is it not beautiful, Excellency?'

'Yes, too beautiful.'

'It is the only one in the world!' smiled the man. 'And I am the inventor.'

'The only one in the world?'

'I swear it!'

'Who else knows of this?'

'No-one. Not even my wife, who would think me mad with the sun. She thought I was making a kite. I rose in the night and walked to the cliffs far away. And when the morning breezes blew and the sun rose, I gathered my courage, Excellency, and leaped from the cliff. I flew! But my wife does not know of it.'

'Well for her, then,' said the Emperor. 'Come along.'

They walked back to the great house. The sun was full in the sky now, and the smell of the grass was refreshing. The Emperor, the servant, and the flier paused within the huge garden.

The Emperor clapped his hands. 'Ho, guards!'

The guards came running.

'Hold this man.'

The guards seized the flier.

'Call the executioner,' said the Emperor.

'What's this!' cried the flier, bewildered. 'What have I done?' He began to weep, so that the beautiful paper apparatus rustled.

'Here is the man who has made a certain machine,' said the Emperor, 'and yet asks us what he has created. He does not know himself. It is only necessary that he create, without knowing why he has done so, or what this thing will do.'

The executioner came running with a sharp silver axe. He stood with his naked, large-muscled arms ready, his face covered with a serene white mask.

'One moment,' said the Emperor. He turned to a nearby table upon which sat a machine that he himself had created.

The Emperor took a tiny golden key from his own neck. He fitted this key to the tiny, delicate machine and wound it up. Then he set the machine going.

The machine was a garden of metal and jewels. Set in motion, birds sang in tiny metal trees, wolves walked through miniature forests, and tiny people ran in and out of sun and shadow, fanning themselves with miniature fans, listening to the tiny emerald birds, and standing by impossibly small but tinkling fountains.

'Is it not beautiful?' said the Emperor. 'If you asked me what I have done here, I could answer you well. I have made birds sing, I have made forests murmur, I have set people to walking in this woodland, enjoying the leaves and shadows and songs. That is what I have done.'

'But, oh, Emperor!' pleaded the flier, on his knees, the tears pouring down his face. 'I have done a similar thing! I have found beauty. I have flown on the morning wind. I have looked down on all the sleeping houses and gardens. I have smelled the sea and even seen it, beyond the hills, from my high place. And I have soared like a bird; oh, I cannot say how beautiful it is up there, in the sky, with the wind about me, the wind blowing me here like a feather, there like a fan, the way the sky smells in the morning! And how free one feels! That is beautiful, Emperor, that is beautiful too!'

'Yes,' said the Emperor sadly, 'I know it must be true. For I felt my heart move with you in the air and I wondered: What is it like? How does it feel? How do the distant pools look from so high? And how my houses and servants? Like ants? And how the distant towns not yet awake?'

'Then spare me!'

'But these are times,' said the Emperor, more sadly still, 'when one must lose a little beauty if one is to keep what little beauty one already has. I do not fear you, yourself, but I fear another man.'

'What man?'

'Some other man who, seeing you, will build a thing of bright papers and bamboo like this. But the other man will have an evil face and an evil heart, and the beauty will be gone. It is this man I fear.'

'Why? Why?'

'Who is to say that someday just such a man, in just such an apparatus of paper and reed, might not fly in the sky and drop huge stones upon the Great Wall of China?' said the Emperor.

No-one moved or said a word.

'Off with his head,' said the Emperor.

The executioner whirled his silver axe.

'Burn the kite and the inventor's body and bury their ashes together,' said the Emperor.

The servants retreated to obey.

The Emperor turned to his hand-servant, who had seen the man flying. 'Hold your tongue. It was all a dream, a most sorrowful and beautiful dream. And that farmer in the distant field who also saw, tell him it would pay him to consider it only a vision. If ever the word passes around, you and the farmer die within the hour.'

'You are merciful, Emperor.'

'No, not merciful,' said the old man. Beyond the garden wall he saw the guards burning the beautiful machine of paper and reeds that smelled of the morning wind. He saw the dark smoke climb into the sky. 'No, only very much bewildered and afraid.' He saw the guards digging a tiny pit wherein to bury the ashes. 'What is the life of one man against those of a million others? I must take solace from that thought.'

He took the key from its chain about his neck and once more wound up the beautiful miniature garden. He stood looking out across the land at the Great Wall, the peaceful town, the green fields, the rivers and streams. He sighed. The tiny garden whirred its hidden and delicate machinery and set itself in motion; tiny people walked in forests, tiny foxes loped through sun-speckled glades in beautiful shining pelts, and among the tiny trees flew little bits of high song and bright blue and yellow colour, flying, flying, flying in that small sky.

'Oh,' said the Emperor, closing his eyes, 'look at the birds, look at the birds!'

Group work – exploration

1. Once you have read the story, talk about it in your group for a few minutes, and then write down your thoughts on the following questions, using the story to help you.

(a) Why did the Emperor call for his guards to execute the flier?

(b) Do you agree with the Emperor's concerns?

(c) What would you have done if you had been the Emperor?

2. Share your answers with the people in your group, taking turns to read what you have written. Then talk about the second question and make a group list of reasons why you **do** agree that the Emperor was sensible to destroy all traces of the Flying Machine (including its creator), and a list of reasons why your group **does not** agree that he did the right thing.

3. When your lists are complete, summarise them as a statement for the whole class to share. Your group must decide, on the evidence you have in your lists, whether the Emperor acted wisely or foolishly.

4. Answer the following questions in your groups, preparing written statements for a full class discussion.

(a) What do you think was Ray Bradbury's purpose in writing 'The Flying Machine'?

(b) What comment on human nature is he making?

(c) Why do you think Bradbury set the story in China in AD 400?

5. After the discussion listen to your teacher read the following essay by Cassandra, the newspaper columnist. He wrote this essay in the *Daily Mirror*.

It's the Letrit!

March 7, 1958

I oppose electricity. Whether the stuff will continue to exist after my condemnation is problematical.

I learned to loathe electricity many, many years ago. An old car I once owned broke down and had to be towed into a garage.

The mechanic was an ancient chap who was probably brought up on steam cars and attributed all the troubles of the motoring world to electricity. He was probably right.

He took one look at my paralysed four-wheeled hulk and said with scorn and dislike: 'Betcha it's the letrit!'

Try pronouncing the word 'electric' as 'letrit'! It is very satisfying.

It gets the real note of contempt that all true electricity loathers feel about the stuff.

He opened the bonnet, pointed to the petrol pump and spat out the word 'Letrit!'

He jabbed an accusing finger at the distributor and snarled: 'Letrit!'

He looked at the fuse-box and found it guilty with one word: 'Letrit!'

He glared at the starter motor and said: 'Letrit!'

He sneered at the headlights and jeered: 'Letrit!'

Then he gave his all-embracing verdict: 'Letrit! Letrit! Letrit! Nothing but this pesky Letrit! No good will come of it, mark my words.'

And no good has come of it.

'Letrit' has not helped this world.

Without 'Letrit!' we would be free from television. Without 'Letrit!' we could be emancipated from the telephone. Without 'Letrit!' we could escape radio, aeroplanes, high-voltage guitars, hairdryers, buzzing razors, neon signs, guided missiles and simply enormous shocks that amateurs like myself receive when we try to put a new plug on the vacuum cleaner.

We could also have fewer newspapers because with the 'Letrit!' one printing machine alone can belt out 60 000 copies an hour.

When I start my own newspaper it will be powered by a water wheel with the splashing of the stream drowning the noise of the horses clip-clopping up to take away the first edition.

When we on the Water-Wheel Press wish to communicate with anyone we will have no telephone so we will put our hat and our coat on and we will summon the four-in-hand to take us to our informants.

Megaphones and ear trumpets will be available for those who just wish to gather the news by sitting and shouting at the passers-by from open windows.

Down with 'letrit!'

---

6. Although Cassandra leaves us in no doubt about his attitude to electricity in this essay, his opinion will probably not be shared by all the people in your class. In your group, talk about:

(a) the uses for electricity that you have, every day, at home and at school, and discuss

(b) whether you think Cassandra's opinion in this essay is serious, or whether he wants to make us smile by taking that particular point of view.

7. Make some notes about your thoughts on the following question.
    'How would our lives be different if we had no electricity?'
   Share these with the people in your group.

8. Now read through the words to Cat Stevens' song 'Where Do the Children Play?'

Where Do the Children Play?

Well I think it's fine building Jumbo planes,
or taking a ride on a cosmic train, switch on
summer from a slot machine, yes get what you
want to, if you want, cause you can get anything.
I know we've come a long way, we're changing day to day,
but tell me, where do the children play?

Well you roll on roads over fresh green grass,
for your lorry loads pumping petrol gas, and you
make them long and you make them tough, but they
just go on and on, and it seems that you can't
get off. Oh, I know we've come a long way,
we're changing day to day, but tell me where
do the children play?

Well you've cracked the sky, scrapers fill the air,
But will you keep on building higher 'til there's
no more room up there. Will you make us laugh,
will you make us cry, will you tell us when to live,
will you tell us when to die. I know we've come a long
way, we're changing day to day. But tell me,
where do the children play?

Cat Stevens

9. Discuss this song in your group so that you are all sure that you understand what it means.

10. Then write down your own ideas about the following questions:

Do you think the repetition of 'Where do the children play?' is a good way to make us consider the **cost** of progress?

What other questions could Cat Stevens have asked in the chorus to this song?

Discussion

You will now have read three pieces of writing on the **theme of progress.** You have talked and thought about progress and the price we pay for it. Here are some topics concerned with this theme that you could discuss:

- The Emperor made the right decision.
- We pay too great a price for progress.
- The advantages of progress outweigh the disadvantages.
- The world would be a better place without nuclear energy.
- The motor car is a mistake.
- We should hasten slowly.

Some approaches

Whole class work

Your teacher might organise a whole class discussion on one or more of the topics.

Group work

Your teacher might arrange for two groups to be given the same topic. The first group would agree with the topic and the other group would have to disagree. Both sides would have to prepare their cases very thoroughly.

When both groups are ready, the side agreeing with the topic would explain their case first. Then the other group would say why they disagreed. The rest of the class could judge who has the stronger arguments.

Remember that you may not be arguing your personal opinion. You will have to take the side that you have been given.

Individual work – writing

Prepare a written argument for your teacher, examining any of the topics from one side only. Use evidence collected from your own research and from what you have heard in discussion. Alternatively, you could write on another topic of your choice concerned with the theme of progress.

Pairs work

Prepare and perform an interview in pairs, one person stating one side of the argument while the other person attempts to make the first person change their mind, **or**

Write this argument in pairs, taking it in turns to respond to what the other person has said.

Poetry writing

Try turning 'The Flying Machine' into a ballad, telling the story in verse. You could set your ballad to music if you can find a tune that would suit.

Survey

Conduct a survey among adults to find out about people's attitudes to change. You will need to think carefully about what questions you will ask. Two possible questions are:

What changes have you seen in your lifetime?

What would you not have believed could happen?

Even in your own lifetime you will have experienced changes – mostly technological changes. List all the items that are available to people now that you can remember as 'new'.

Present the findings of your survey and your own thoughts on change to the class.

Film

The Flying Machine, U.S., 1979. Directed by Bernard Selling. Before seeing the film, re-read the story so that it is fresh in your mind. Then, in your groups:

- Make a list of the similarities and differences between the film and the story.

- Discuss what you have learned about how to change a short story into a film.

- Be prepared to share your ideas in a full class discussion on these topics.

Reflection

Spend ten minutes writing in your journal about the work you have done in this chapter.

- What thoughts and feelings about progress do you have after focusing on this topic?

- What worries you most about the progress human kind has made?

- What do you find most pleasant or attractive about progress?

'Here is the man who has made a certain machine,' said the Emperor, 'and yet asks us what he has created.' He does not know himself. It is only necessary that he create, without knowing why he has done so, or what this thing will do.'

Can you think of any ways in which this statement can be applied to the modern world?

Further reading

Joy Adamson, *Born Free*
Richard Carpenter, *Catweazle*
Peter Dickinson, *The Devil's Children*
Jean George, *My Side of the Mountain*
Patricia Wrightson, *An Older Kind of Magic,*
   The Nargun and the Stars

When the Indians

When the Indians
Sold
New York
For a handsome
Sum of
Glass beads,
They scouted west
And crossed
What is now called
The Mississippi,
Travelling west
On what is now called
Route 66
Until they arrived at
What is now called
California.
They decided to
Sell this too
For what is now
Called money,
But the whites
Took it with
What is now called
Guns.

William Eastlake

9 Drama script: the play's opening

The activities in this chapter are designed to help you to look closely at a drama script and to understand how playwrights develop their characters. This should provide a good introduction for you to write your own plays.

The chapter contains the opening scene from Robert Bolt's play *The Thwarting of Baron Bolligrew*. Reading and acting out the script should be fun, and you might even want to look at the whole play when you have finished this chapter.

The Thwarting of Baron Bolligrew
by *Robert Bolt*

Cast

Storyteller
Duke
Sir Digby Vayne-Trumpington
First Knight
Sir Graceless Strongbody
Sir Percival Smoothely-Smoothe
Sir Oblong fitz Oblong
Juniper
Other Knights
Captain

ACT I

The Curtain *rises on a stage which is dark except for a single spot down* C, *in which stands the* Storyteller. *He wears something unique, to set him apart.*

Storyteller   A long time ago – in the days when dragons were still common – there lived a Duke. And whenever news was brought in of a dragon ravaging some part of the country the Duke sent one of his Knights away in shining armour to deal with it. After a few weeks the Knight would return with the tip of the dragon's tail to

prove that he had killed it. Dragons are excessively vain, and when the tips of their tails are cut off they die, of mulligrubs. The return of the Knights would be announced like this:

(A fanfare sounds. The Lights *come up, revealing a stage bare of scenery except for drapes and a cyclorama. At a round table sit the* Duke *and the* Knights. *The* Duke *is an elderly, well-fed aristocrat, well-meaning and indolent. He wears civilian garb, fairy-tale period. The* Knights *wear armour, except for* Juniper, *who wears less magnificent civvies than the Duke. They wear surcoats bearing the Royal Shawberry. The seat on Duke's* L *is vacant, and other empty ones are to be seen round the table)*

(Moving to one side and announcing) Sir Digby Vayne-Trumpington!

*(*Trumpington *enters)*

Duke   Ah, there you are, Trumpington. Glad to have you back. Got the tip of the dragon's tail?

*(*Trumpington *places the bright blue tail-tip on the table. The* Duke *inspects it)*

Not very big, is it?

Trumpington   It was not a large dragon, Your Grace, no; but singularly vicious.

First Knight   They can be tricky, those little blue beggars.

(There is a murmur of agreement)

Duke   Not complaining, Trumpington. We can't all be St Georges, can we?

(While Trumpington *sits, there is a fanfare)*

Storyteller   Sir Graceless Strongbody!

(There is a pause all looking off expectantly)

Duke   *(indulgently)* Likes to make an entrance, Strongbody . . . *(The pause continues. Less indulgently)* Call him again.
Sir Grace . . . !

*(*Strongbody *enters dragging a huge green tail. Murmurs of appreciation and then polite clapping come from the* Knights)*

Duke   I must *say*, Graceless! I think we'll have this stuffed, gentlemen. How d'you do it?

Strongbody   *(gruffly)* Oh, usual methods, ye know.

Duke   Aha – 'Deeds not Words', the old Strongbody motto.
(There is another fanfare)

Storyteller   Sir Percival Smoothely-Smoothe!

(Smoothe enters)

Duke Good show, Smoothe; back on time as usual. Find your dragon?

(Smoothe puts down two red tail-tips)

Good Lord, *two* dragons!

Smoothe No, Your Grace, one dragon with two tails.

Duke Well I never saw such a thing in my life. Gave you a bit of trouble I dare say?

Smoothe *(sitting)* Not really, Your Grace. It seemed to be confused.

Duke Ah, modest, modest. I like that, Smoothe, like it. Well now, who's missing? *(Looking at the vacant seat to his L.)* Oh, Oblong. Not like him to be late. Well we'll just wait for Oblong, gentlemen, and then I have a little announcement to make, yes . . .

(There is another fanfare)

Storyteller Sir Oblong fitz Oblong!

(Sir Oblong fitz Oblong enters sadly. He is short, plump, with a pink innocent face topped by a tonsure of white hair. He is pedantic and almost priggy, and wears silver armour)

Duke There you are, Oblong; mission accomplished?

Oblong Yes, Your Grace.

Duke Got the tail?

Oblong Yes, Your Grace.

Duke *(kindly)* Well perk up, man. Whatever's the matter?

Oblong *(producing a tail)* It was a very small dragon, Your Grace. Small and, er pink. I don't think it can have been fully grown. It meant no harm I'm sure. *(He regards the small pink tail on table, then takes a handkerchief from the sleeve of his armour and blows his nose)*

Duke Now Oblong, we all know how you feel about animals, and I'm sure respect you for it. *(He looks round)*

(There is a murmur of confirmation from the Knights*)*

But – Duty First, eh?

Oblong *(bracing)* Yes, Your Grace. *(He sits L of Duke)*

Duke That's it. *(Patting Oblong's shoulder as he sits)* Never knew an Oblong hold back in the face of duty. *(Briskly)* Now, Juniper my dear chap, read the next item on the agenda will you?

Juniper Er, 'Activities for the coming Season', Your Grace.

Duke Exactly! *(Rising)* Gentlemen, a happy announcement: There *are* no activities for the coming season. These *(the tails on the table)* were the last dragons in the Dukedom. Thanks to your untiring efforts over the years our peasantry may now reap their harvests – and pay their taxes – without interference. Our townsfolk can make their profits – and pay their taxes freely. And in short, there isn't a blessed thing for us to do.

(The Knights *rise and congratulate one another noisily shaking hands, patting backs, etc. The hubbub dies and they all sit)*

Oblong	How perfectly splendid, Your Grace.
Duke	Isn't it, isn't it?
Oblong	Now we can move on somewhere else.
Duke	*(faintly)* Er, 'move on', Oblong?
Oblong	Yes, Your Grace.
Duke	Whatever for?
Oblong	*(mildly puzzled)* To succour the poor and needy, Your Grace. Up North, for instance – dragons, barons, goblins. Having a very thin time of it up North, the poor and needy.
Duke	But my dear fellow – the climate!
Oblong	Well, South, then, Your Grace.
Smoothe	*(gently)* May I say something, Your Grace?
Duke	Smoothe! Yes! Please, please.
Smoothe	Well gentlemen, we've put this district into some sort of shape – and it's not been easy as you know. It seems to me we've earned a breather.
Duke	Earned a breather. Well said, Smoothe. Late lie-in in the morning. Bit of jousting in the afternoon perhaps. Substantial supper; jolly good game of musical bumps and off to bed. *(Appealing all round)* Where's the harm in that?

(A murmur of considered agreement)

I'll put it to the vote. Democratic procedure – Can't say fairer than that, Oblong. All those in favour of the programme just outlined, please say 'Aye'.

All but Oblong	Aye!
Duke	Thank you. All those in favour of moving on, to wild, wet, baron and dragon infested areas, please say 'Aye'.
Oblong	Er, Aye.
Duke	*(cheerfully)* Well there it is, old man. You're outvoted.
Oblong	*(diffident)* Under the terms of our Charter, Your Grace, I *think* a vote on this subject has to be unanimous. Nobody must disagree.
Duke	*(weakly)* That right?
Juniper	*(looking at the Charter on the table)* I'm just looking . . . Yes, here it is, Your Grace, Clause Seven. *(He passes the Charter to the Duke)*
Duke	Well . . . *(Petulantly)* Very ill-judged Clause, I would say. Now what?
Juniper	If we can't agree, Your Grace, we must refer the matter to the Royal Court.

Strongbody	*(gloomily)* And we know what they'll say . . .
Oblong	I'm sorry to be the fly in the ointment, gentlemen, but – to succour the poor and needy – dash it all gentlemen, it's our Knightly Vow!

(At this, All look uncomfortably at the table. The small pink tail twitches slowly in the silence. All look. Oblong is distressed)

Oh dear; Your Grace, would you mind . . .

Duke	*(testy)* Yes, yes, take it away if it upsets you: take them *all* away.

(Oblong rises and picks up the tails)

Oblong	*(muttering; embarrassed)* 'Scuse me, gentlemen – I – *(He moves to go, then turns. Apologetically)* – er – oh dear . . .

(Oblong exits with the tails, watched by all)

Juniper	Well, there goes the late lie-in.
Strongbody	And the joustin'.
Trumpington	And the musical bumps.
Juniper	And the substantial suppers.
First Knight	*(uneasy)* Got a point there, you know, about the Knightly Vow.
Duke	Yes, yes; capital creature; heart of gold; but . . .
Smoothe	But inclined to be dogmatic, Your Grace.
Duke	Exactly.
Smoothe	I think I see a possible solution.

(All raise their heads and look to Smoothe)

Supposing Oblong were to leave us. On a mission. A mission to – say – the Bolligrew Islands.

Duke	The Bolligrew Islands!
First Knight	I say, that's a bit steep.
Trumpington	D'you think he'd go?
Juniper	It's worth trying. Your Grace might have him appointed a Royal Knight Errant.
Duke	And then when he'd gone we could put the matter to the vote again and – er . . .?
Juniper	And nobody would disagree!
Duke	Unanimous vote, as required by our Charter!
Smoothe	Exactly, Your Grace.
Duke	*(solemnly)* There's no doubt, gentlemen, the Bolligrew Islands *need* a Knight Errant.
Juniper	Unquestionably.
Duke	And Oblong is the obvious choice.
First Knight	That's true.
Duke	I dare say he'll be very happy there.

(Smoothe coughs warningly. Oblong enters)

	Oblong my dear chap, what would you say to the idea of a mission to the Bolligrew Islands?
Oblong	I should say it was a very *good* idea, Your Grace! When do we start?
Duke	Well, we were thinking of a – more of a – one man mission, you know.
Oblong	Oh. Me?
Duke	Yes. Smoothe here suggested you.
Oblong	*(sharply)* Very good of you, Smoothe. I'm not going.
Duke	'Not', Oblong?
Oblong	No! The Bolligrew Islands! That's where Baron Bolligrew lives – the one that pulled down the church!
Duke	*(shocked)* Did he really? I didn't know that.
Oblong	Well he did. And there's that dragon in the Bolligrew Islands too.
Smoothe	A very *poor* specimen, I believe.
Oblong	It isn't. It's one of those black ones with red eyes.
First Knight	*(uncomfortably)* It's a bit steep, you know.
Smoothe	Quite right, quite right. We ought not to persuade Sir Oblong.

(Oblong moves to his chair but is stopped by Smoothe's next words)

	It is a pity, though. I understand that Baron Bolligrew hunts.
Oblong	*(sharply)* Hunts?
Smoothe	*(looking up in mock surprise)* Er, hunts, yes.
Oblong	*(suspiciously)* What does he hunt?
Smoothe	*(looking to the Duke)* Pretty well anything, they say.
Duke	Foxes.
Smoothe	*(nodding)* Foxes, bears –
Trumpington	Deer –
Juniper	Badgers –
Oblong	Oh the villain!
Smoothe	*(offhand)* Hares, of course – little, trembling hares . . .
Oblong	It – really it makes one's blood boil!
Smoothe	Your Grace, if Sir Oblong *were* going on this mission I expect His Majesty would make him a Royal Knight Errant, don't you?
Duke	Couldn't refuse. And then you could wear the purple robe, you know, with the Royal Coat of Arms and so on. I think Oblong would look well in purple, don't you, Juniper?
Oblong	*(taken with it)* Really? I must say – hares and badgers you say?
Smoothe	Oh anything.
Oblong	The perfect brute! Your Grace, I'll go.
Duke	Excellent conclusion to a good morning's work, gentlemen. How about a little refreshment?
Storyteller	Lemonade and ice-cream on the South Terrace!
Duke	Meeting adjourned!

(The Duke *and* Knights *exit, rolling the table with them. The* Lights *go out, except for the single spot* C *as the* Storyteller *moves below it)*

Storyteller   So Sir Oblong was appointed a Royal Knight Errant and at length –

(A brown paper parcel is thrown on from wings and caught by the Storyteller)

– a parcel from the King's Court arrived at the Duke's Castle – *(he opens the parcel)* – containing Sir Oblong's purple robe.

(Oblong enters into the spot, and is assisted into the robe by the Storyteller)

Sir Oblong put it on and he found a berth on a ship –

(The Captain *enters carrying a 'mast and sail')*

– which was making the short but dangerous passage to the Bolligrew Islands.

Group work – exploring the scene

Discuss these questions in your group.

1. What do you learn from the opening scene:

    about the world in which the play takes place?

    about the kind of play this will be?

    about the characters? Concentrate especially on Oblong, the Duke, Smoothe and Baron Bolligrew.

2. Smoothe and Oblong have different opinions about the dragon on the Bolligrew Islands. Whom do you believe? Why?

3. Who are likely to be the main characters in the play?

4. Will the play have a happy ending?

Group work – characterisation

We learn about the kinds of people the various characters are in a number of ways:

what they say

what they do

what others say about them

what they wear and what they look like.

In this extract Robert Bolt gives readers of his script clues to the sorts of people that the Duke and Oblong are just before they make their first appearance. Sometimes names give us clues about characters as well.

From the information provided in the script we can build up character profiles of these four people:

- Oblong
- the Duke
- Smoothe
- Baron Bolligrew

Your teacher will divide the class into four groups, so that each group has one character profile to complete.

Building up a character profile

Your task:

Using the above information about characterisation, look at the play and write a profile of your character. The profile should contain the following information about your character:

- appearance
- strengths
- weaknesses
- what other people think of him

When you have finished preparing your profile, your teacher will help you to form new groups containing four people, each with a different character profile. Pass these profiles around the group, and discuss any similarities and differences that you note.

Individual or pairs work – writing

Write a short scene that you imagine could occur later in the play, *The Thwarting of Baron Bolligrew*. Robert Bolt has already given some clues about what will or might happen later. What are these clues? Use these, or imagine your own adventures for Oblong.

A suggested approach

Writing for the theatre is difficult and certainly very different from most other kinds of writing. What you write must be able to be acted out and must work on the stage.

Look at the way Robert Bolt has written the opening scene of the play. In your scene see if you can use some of these features of writing drama:

- Give some information about the **characters** when they appear for the first time. Robert Bolt gives information about what the Duke and Oblong look like and what sort of people they are just before they first appear.

- Give some **stage directions** to the actors about their actions, their movements and, when necessary, how they should speak their lines.

- Include some **sound effects**.

- Give details of the **costumes** to be worn and any special effects to be used.

- Make sure you keep to the form that writers use for drama:

    Names of characters are placed before their dialogue.

    No inverted commas are used for speech.

    Start a new line for each character's dialogue.

    When you give stage directions, leave a line before and after the directions so that they are set apart from the dialogue.

    Consider writing your stage directions in a different colour so that they stand out.

Check carefully through the extract from *The Thwarting of Baron Bolligrew* to see that you have the dramatic form correct.

Give your script to another group to perform for the class. You can judge how successful your script writing has been by how well 'your' actors handle your script.

Further reading

If you're interested in reading about dragons you might enjoy:
J. R. R. Tolkien, *The Hobbit*
Ursula Le Guin, *The Wizard of Earthsea*
Rosemary Sutcliff, *Dragonslayer*

10 Point of view: where the writer stands

This chapter is designed to help you understand the way different authors **choose** to look at life in a certain way, so that they can force the reader to look at things that way too. You will learn how they do this, and you will practise using different ways of looking at the world in your own writing.

Here are three poems for you to read. They are very different from each other, but are all written in the first person (with the poet becoming the narrator and so using the pronoun 'I').

1. Read the poems through to yourself. Write down whom or what you think the **narrator** is in each poem.

Street Boy

Just you look at me, man,
Stompin' down the street
My crombie stuffed with biceps
My boots is filled with feet.

Just you hark to me, man,
When they call us out
My head is full of silence
My mouth is full of shout.

Just you watch me move, man,
Steady like a clock
My heart is spaced on blue beat
My soul is stoned on rock.

Just you read my name, man,
Writ for all to see
The walls is red with stories
The streets is filled with me.

Gareth Owen

Arithmetic

I'm 11. And I don't really know
my Two Times Table. Teacher says it's disgraceful
But even if I had the time, I feel too tired.
Ron's 5, Samantha's 3, Carole's 18 months,
and then there's Baby. I do what's required.

Mum's working, Dad's away. And so
I dress them, give them breakfast. Mrs Russell
moves in, and I take Ron to school.
Miss Eames calls me an old-fashioned word: Dunce.
Doreen Maloney says I'm fool.

After tea, to the Rec. Pram-pushing's slow
but on fine days it's a good place, full
of larky boys. When 6 shows on the clock
I put the kids to bed. I'm free for once.
At about 7 – Mum's key in the lock.

Gavin Ewart

The Lonely Scarecrow

My poor old bones – I've only two –
A broomshank and a broken stave.
My ragged gloves are a disgrace.
My one peg-foot is in the grave.

I wear the labourer's old clothes:
Coat, shirt and trousers all undone.
I bear my cross upon a hill
In rain and shine, in snow and sun.

I cannot help the way I look.
My funny hat is full of hay.
– O, wild birds, come and nest in me!
Why do you always fly away?

James Kirkup

2. Perhaps someone in the class will volunteer to read these poems aloud for you to enjoy. Share your ideas about who you think the narrator is in each poem.

3. Now think about the expression, **point of view**. Talk about it in your group, and see if you can come up with a definition of the term, point of view, as you understand it.

4. Give your group's definition to your teacher, who will write the definitions from all the groups onto the blackboard.

5. Read through all the definitions the class has come up with, and discuss any that you think are different from the rest, until you agree on the best definition.

Here is a story that is written from one person's point of view. The story is Jonathan Dawson's 'Aunt Jane'. Your teacher will read the story to you.

Just from the title, can you guess from whose point of view the story will be written?

Aunt Jane
by *Jonathan Dawson*

In the late summer of 1905, David Nimmo's unmarried Aunt Jane came to take him away for a holiday by the sea. Even though David was an appraising nine, Jane seemed extraordinarily young for an Aunt, slim and poised like a bird with eager brown hands and a small tilted head.

'How well you look Jane, and how alive.' His mother kissed her on both cheeks as they left. Mrs Nimmo already seemed middle-aged and tired, although they had servants, and only her eyes showed that she was Jane's sister. David liked his Aunt's bright clothes, like pictures from the English magazines his father brought up from the town.

They rattled away in clouds of dust, high in Aunt Jane's motor (which no one really approved of) and David felt just a little sorry as the last glimpse of the red roof disappeared through the dry white gums. After a while they stopped for tea at the nearby town.

'We're only a few miles from Melbourne now,' said Aunt Jane. David felt not at all shy, and they sipped tea and ate huge creamy cakes as the smell of eucalyptus blew in on them through the lace curtains of the small tea-rooms. Another motor drew up with a rattle and a tall young man came in and sat at the next table. David saw that he had white patches around his eyes from his driving goggles and he was smoking a long white cigarette in a holder.

'Smoking is for fools,' David's father had said. 'It ruins the heart.' David looked curiously at the young man, but he seemed well enough.

The young man turned slightly in his chair and looked carefully at Aunt Jane. First her face, David noted, then at the brooch on her dress. The dress seemed very low to David, his mother always wore hers high and nudged father in church when the store-keeper's daughter came in with a dress like Aunt Jane's. Her skin was very brown and soft, and swelled slightly above the lace part.

She turned and noticed the young man and a faint flush tinged her skin. David wanted to squeeze her she looked so warm, and he felt absurdly happy.

When they got up to leave David smiled at the young motorist, but pale rimmed eyes swung to follow Aunt Jane as they went out the door.

'Did you see that man?' asked David. 'He had a car just like yours. Are there many cars in Melbourne?'

'Lots of cars,' Aunt Jane said absently, half turning her head towards the door, but the wind caught a loose lock of her high piled hair and she flicked a quick brown hand at it impatiently as they climbed into the car. The tea-room man swung the crank, they waved, and were off.

Melbourne was so big and coloured, so unreal with its packed and noisy tramcars, sounds of engines and voices, and the tall buildings with great windows and striped awnings above the pavement shops. David wanted to stop and see everything but it was late, the yellow street lamps already slowly lighting, and they rolled on through the wide streets and out down the long line of trees and white houses of St Kilda Road.

'Not far to go,' shouted Aunt Jane above the wind and roar, but David was not tired at all, and he watched the rows of tall trees turn gold in the setting sun, then back to a strange green as the lights came on, and once, looking back, he saw the black silhouettes of city buildings lined by electric light and the squat shapes of trams filled with tall elegant people.

Then they swept onto the coast road and David could at last see the sea, as he had pictured it, dark and heaving, touched lightly with a thousand movements as the sun slid irregularly out of sight.

The Guest House was dark, smelling of carpets and salt, brass and dinner. When the roar of the motor left his ears, David could at last hear the slow roll and hiss of the sea. The trees outside their room tossed in a chill salt wind.

'Did you see the man with the motor?' asked David. 'He had dinner at the table on the other side of the room. Do you think he is staying here too?'

'No,' said Aunt Jane, 'no, I didn't see him.'

The morning wind outside the window blew in the sun and the crisp nervous air. For a moment David missed the familiar sweetness of the eucalyptus, but then the sudden pull and rush of a wave woke him to the sea nearby and he rushed to the window to pull aside curtains sharp with salt. In a moment Aunt Jane came in, already fully dressed, her hair drawn tightly back from her face making her eyes even larger. She was holding a wide straw hat piled with flowers.

'Come on David,' she said, 'time for breakfast.' They went down the dark polished stairs to the smell and clatter of toast and eggs.

As soon as breakfast was over they left the Guest House and

walked down to the sound of the sea. The beach was already mushroomed with umbrellas, and people popped like jacks from the striped bathing boxes to dash into the spray. Along the long promenade the fashionable ladies walked with young men wearing striped blazers and swinging canes, and the older ladies, circular in furs and hung with crepe flowers, paraded small snapping dogs (quite unlike the panting blue cattle dogs of home). And best of all, far out to sea, David could see the thin lazily-dipping funnels of a steam boat swelling out of his books and moving into reality. He ran swooping along the promenade past the marching poodles and looked back to see Aunt Jane waving and laughing, her head tilted, her teeth white in the sun. He almost collided with the young man.

'Careful there David,' he said as he sidestepped. 'You should sound your horn.' The young man was very tall, and wore a boater with a striped ribbon and a white-coloured jacket.

'How did you know my name sir?' said David with admirable presence of mind.

'Oh, I heard your mother call you David in the teashop,' said the tall young man. 'And my name is William Everton Blainey. How do you do.' He bent heroically from the waist.

'That's not my mother, it's my Aunt Jane,' explained David, 'and my name is David Nimmo and I really should go back now.'

'Well, I'll walk back with you,' said the young man, and they strolled slowly back along the promenade towards Aunt Jane.

She looked rather surprised as they came up, and David saw the same red movement along her throat.

'Please accept my apologies for intruding,' said the tall young man. 'But David here nearly ran me down, and I thought I should return him. My name is Bill Blainey.'

'Thank you so much Mr Blainey,' said Aunt Jane evenly. 'Come along David, after lunch we shall bathe.'

The young man smiled and sauntered off down to the beach. David caught Aunt Jane looking absently after him.

'A swim,' she repeated, 'a swim after lunch.'

That evening Mr Blainey appeared suddenly at the dinner table.

'Please excuse me once more,' he said, 'but do you mind if I join you. I know absolutely no one here and it can be very boring all alone. I'm sure you find it so.'

Aunt Jane laughed. 'I'm certain you have no trouble in finding acquaintances Mr – er – Everton. But do join us by all means. David, would you introduce us? I have absolutely no time for the long and tedious processes of making acquaintances so we should be pleased to have you join us. David.'

'Mr William Everton Blainey, Aunt Jane Barton.' They all laughed.

'I must admit,' said Aunt Jane, 'I don't know a soul here either, but David is very good company.'

'I'm sure he is,' said Mr Blainey. 'He nearly bowled me over the first time he bumped into me.' And they all laughed again.

That night they all went to the pier to hear the band. Everybody was laughing and talking at the top of their voices, and nobody seemed to mind at all when a redfaced young man singing at the end of the pier, swayed and suddenly fell with a loud splash into the shallow water to emerge a few minutes later dripping and laughing in the arms of another equally soaked young man. Aunt Jane and Mr Blainey thought this very funny, and indeed to David it seemed that he had never seen so many people happy before. The band blared and strummed on a stand at the end of the pier, the blasts of sound almost drowned by the noise of the crowds, and David noticed that the tuba player, a huge fat man sweating in his gold and blue, was drinking something from a bottle and shouting to the crowd between blasts on his gleaming instrument.

David's head swam with the noise but Aunt Jane and Mr Blainey, arm in arm and talking at the top of their voices, hardly seemed to notice. He turned away for a minute, and caught sight of a small crowd of men in vivid cravats and with great silver watch-chains shouting and urging on a young couple struggling with each other under the pier lights. The girl, half laughing, half crying, was trying to fight off the man, who, with his arms tight around her was trying to kiss her. His face looked oddly yellow and twisted in the artificial light and David suddenly felt quite frightened; he did not understand. He turned quickly back as a roar went up from the men, and he ran back to Aunt Jane who was talking earnestly to Mr Blainey.

'What's the matter David dear,' she said. 'Oh god, I am selfish, come on Bill, we'll take him back at once.' Mr Blainey sighed, but winked at David as they began to hurry back to the Guest House, jostled by the crowds, deafened by the noise.

The next day they went out on the pleasure steamer, and it was the happiest day of David's life. The sea was calm and absurdly blue, and the soft thud of the engines seemed part of the slow swell of the water. Aunt Jane and Mr Blainey were talking and laughing together all the time, so David could examine the boat from stem to stern. He watched the boiling rush behind, the parted spray at the bows, the sea gliding past as he hung over the railings, and the immensity of his happiness amazed him. He stared with awe at the splendid captain, who winked back at him from the wheel through his stern black whiskers. And when he looked back, he could see the rows of houses, the beach huts and the umbrellas, and away to his right over the lifeboats, he could see the long green arc of bay, and the dark cluster of Melbourne with its steeples, office buildings and at the edge of the city, the dizzy chimneys drifting smoke. Once with a swoop of whistling and a dash of steam, the pilot boat heeled past heading out to the enormity of the ocean beyond.

That night David slept dreamlessly, his imagination exhausted. He was woken by laughter next door, and presently Aunt Jane and Mr Blainey came to fetch him to breakfast. Mr Blainey's eyes had marks like soot underneath, but Aunt Jane was even more glowing than David had seen her before, her skin had a soft transparent look, and she held onto Mr Blainey's arm very tightly. They laughed a lot during breakfast, even at the things David actually meant as jokes. It was all very satisfactory.

It was then that the very odd thing happened. The waiter came over to the table and whispered in Mr Blainey's ear. He smiled and turned to Aunt Jane.

'Excuse me for a moment Jane, it appears that someone wants to see me, I shan't be a moment.'

The waiter pointed, and David could see a short man with a bowler hat standing by the potted fern at a door. He was staring hard at Mr Blainey who rose smiling and went over to him. They talked for a moment, then Mr Blainey turned and took a long look at Aunt Jane. His face had gone completely white and misshapen like that of the man on the pier and once again David felt frightened without knowing why. Mr Blainey opened his mouth as if to speak, then, with an odd gesture he turned and left the dining-room with the short man trotting beside him holding his arm. Aunt Jane half rose from her seat but said nothing for a moment. Then she sat down.

'David, drink your milk,' she said. Mr Blainey and she had talked so much that she had barely touched her breakfast. Now she just stared at her plate. The sea sounded loud and swift outside.

'Let's go for a bathe early today,' begged David.

Mr Blainey did not reappear all that morning, and Aunt Jane was very quiet and refused to swim. When they came in for lunch one of the promenade ladies, her dog puffing at her feet, was talking loudly at the next table.

'Just imagine,' she shouted to the room, 'three thousand pounds he got away with. But they never get away with it for long. Him living like a lord in this guest house, and his poor wife left alone. A good thing they caught up with him.' Just then her dog started barking and a waiter approached, but Aunt Jane had got up at once, the red fire on her throat, and quickly left the room. David gouged at his salad. Outside the dining-room he could hear in a sudden silence his aunt's voice low and questioning. He decided to ask her if he could have some more ice-cream and salad, but as he came out into the hall he saw her talking to the manager and the sudden expressionlessness of her face made him stop. Abruptly she turned and half ran out of the door and David, for some indefinable reason, decided not to follow her. She did not come back all that afternoon.

At about three o'clock the wind blew a soft spray of rain across the roof and the sea receded greyly. In the guest house the waiter moved around lighting the slow yellow lamps, and the manager organised games for the children in the empty dance room.

At five o'clock a middle-aged man with a sad kindly face (rather like David's father) came in and spoke quickly to the manager. David saw them turn and look at him, and although the strange man's face was kind, he felt again that odd afraid uncertainty.

The next day in the middle of the morning his mother and father came to take him home, and he could see that his mother had been crying. Father held her all the way home and no one spoke, so that although David had so much to tell, especially about the steamboat ride, he decided to wait until they got home.

'Oh why, why?' cried his mother when they got home. 'Why?'

But David's father did not seem to know. Nor would they tell David where Aunt Jane had gone.

The pier had begun to fall into the sea and the guest house was turned into a hospital before he returned to that beach. By then the reasons for the shouts and bustle on the beach that forgotten afternoon were clear.

But however hard he tried, he could remember nothing of his long dead aunt but the quick movement of her hands and the strange swell of her skin just above the lace.

Group work – exploring the story

1. Are there any parts of the story that you don't understand? If you're not sure of any part, read it over again, and discuss the meaning with your group, until you all feel satisfied that you understand the story.

2. Here are some questions to discuss with your group, to help make your understanding of **point of view** clearer:

(a) Who is narrating the story?

(b) From whose point of view is the story told? How can you tell?

(c) Does the writer, Jonathan Dawson, take any part in the story as a character?

   If you have any problems, ask your teacher to join the discussion.

3. Do you understand the difference between the narrator of a story and the person from whose point of view it is told?

Individual work – writing

1. Here are some of the characters from the story:

● Aunt Jane,

● David's mother and father,

● William Everton Blainey,

● the short man with the bowler hat,

● a hotel guest.

   Think about how this story would be different if Jonathan Dawson had told it from the point of view of one of these characters. Share your ideas with the people in your group.

2. Choose a point of view other than David's, and retell the story of Jane from that point of view. You can choose to write from the point of view of any other person in the story. Here are some suggestions of the steps you might take.

(a) Once you have chosen your character, you might need to read the story again, with these points in mind:

● How much information does your character have from his or her point of view?

● Is it the same information that David had?

● If you make up some information that David **didn't** have will it still fit with what David saw and felt?

(b) Make some notes for yourself before you write your first draft, and ask your group for help if you need, so that you can keep to your chosen point of view.

(c) When you're clear about what you can include in the story from your character's point of view, write your first draft, and share it with one other person in your group.

(d) Ask your partner to read your first draft to check that you have kept up your character's point of view, and that your story still makes sense alongside Jonathon Dawson's story.

You may be happy to just write a first draft of your story and leave it at that. However, if you wish to develop the story further, here are some suggestions of ways in which you could present the finished product.

- Combine stories from the points of view of four or more different characters into a book for the school library. You can include Jonathan Dawson's story with yours.

- Make a wall display with a section for each character's point of view, and pin your final draft up in your section for the whole class to read.

- Turn your final drafts into scripts for a taped radio programme, *The Aunt Jane Mystery*. One person could act as the interviewer, and ask each character to tell the story from his or her point of view.

- Send your final drafts, and Jonathan Dawson's original story, to a 5th year class, and ask them to comment on how well you have each written from your chosen point of view.

Can you remember any time in your own life when, like David in this story, you didn't really understand something that was happening? Or have you ever had a dream that you couldn't understand? You might like to spend some time writing about your memory or your dream in your journal. If you want to, you could share what you have written with your group or your teacher, telling the story from your own point of view.

Drawing by C.E.M; 1961
The New Yorker Magazine, Inc.

The following poem by Adrian Mitchell was someone's point of view to show how he deals with people in authority. You might like to try to write a poem that describes a character you know from **their** point of view.

Dumb Insolence

I'm big for ten years old
Maybe that's why they get at me

Teachers, parents, cops
Always getting at me

When they get at me

I don't hit em
They can do you for that

I don't swear at em
They can do you for that

I stick my hands in my pockets
And stare at them

And while I stare at them
I think about sick

They call it dumb insolence

They don't like it
But they can't do you for it

Adrian Mitchell

Reflection

1. In your journal, write your own personal responses to the following questions.

(a) What sort of person do you think Aunt Jane was?

(b) What do you think happened to Aunt Jane?

2. Discuss these questions with the people in your group, and write down your ideas about them for your teacher.

(a) Why do you think Jonathan Dawson chose to tell the story of Aunt Jane from David's point of view?

(b) Think back to the other stories and books you have read this year. Try to decide from what point of view they were written.

● did the author take part in the story as a character?

● did the author tell the story from the point of view of one of the characters?

● did the author know everything about the story and the characters, so that she or he didn't really take the point of view of any single character, but just narrated the story?

3. You might find it interesting to read over some of your own stories, and decide whose point of view you were using.

I share my bedroom with my brother

I share my bedroom with my brother
and I don't like it.
His bed's by the window
under my map of England's railways
that has a hole in just above Leicester
where Tony Sanders, he says,
killed a Roman centurion
with the Radio Times.

My bed's in the corner
and the paint on the skirting board
wrinkles when I push it with my thumb
which I do sometimes when I go to bed
sometimes when I wake up
but mostly on Sundays
when we stay in bed all morning.

That's when he makes pillow dens
under the blankets
so that only his left eye shows
and when I go deep-bed mining
for elastoplast spools
that I scatter with my feet
the night before,
and I jump on to his bed
shouting: eeyoueeyoueeyouee
heaping pillows on his head:
'Now breathe, now breathe'
and then there's quiet and silence
so I pull it away quick
and he's there laughing all over
sucking fresh air along his breathing-tube fingers.

Actually, sharing's all right.

Michael Rosen

The National Union of Children

NUC has just passed a weighty resolution:
'Unless all parents raise our rate of pay
This action will be taken by our members
(The resolution comes in force today): –

'Noses will not be blown (sniffs are in order),
Bedtime will get preposterously late,
Ice-cream and crisps will be consumed for breakfast,
Unwanted cabbage left upon the plate,

'Earholes and fingernails can't be inspected,
Overtime (known as homework) won't be worked,
Reports from school will all say "Could do better",
Putting bricks back in boxes may be shirked.'

The National Association of Parents

Of course, NAP's answer quickly was forthcoming
(It was a matter of emergency),
It issued to the Press the following statement
(Its Secretary appeared upon TV): –

'True that the so-called Saturday allowance
Hasn't kept pace with prices in the shops,
But neither have, alas, parental wages:
NUC's claim would ruin kind, hard-working Pops.

'Therefore, unless that claim is now abandoned,
Strike action for us, too, is what remains;
In planning for the which we are in process
Of issuing, to all our members, canes.'

Roy Fuller

Further reading

If you are interested in seeing how different writers use point
of view, you might enjoy reading some of these books.

Bernard Ashley, *The Trouble with Donovan Croft*
Lynne Reid Banks, *One More River*
Betsy Byars, *The Eighteenth Emergency, The Cartoonist, The
    Pinballs*
Agatha Christie, *The Murder of Roger Ackroyd*
Beverley Cleary, *Dear Mr Henshaw*
Gene Kemp, *The Turbulent Term of Tyke Tyler*
Judith Kerr, *When Hitler Stole Pink Rabbit*
Robin Klein, *Hating Alison Ashley*
Katherine Paterson, *The Great Gilly Hopkins*
Gene Kemp, *The Turbulent Term of Tyke Tyler*
Ivan Southall, *Ash Road, Let the Balloon Go*
Randolph Stow, *Midnite*
Theodore Taylor, *The Cay*
Patricia Wrightson, *I Own the Racecourse*

11 Reading and writing a fantasy novel

The aims of this chapter are:

- to introduce you to the world of fantasy by encouraging you to read or re-read a range of fantasy novels, and

- to enable you to write your own fantasy.

The example used in this chapter is *The Lion, the Witch and the Wardrobe* by C. S. Lewis. It could, however, be easily adapted to any novel which you, or your teacher, decides to use. There is a list of books at the end of this chapter which might be useful.

Did you ever read *The Lion, the Witch and the Wardrobe* in Primary School? If you did, or if your teacher read it to you, then you'll already know about the land of Narnia that lies beyond the wardrobe, and you will most probably welcome the opportunity to re-read this novel through the eyes of an older person. If you've never read the book before then it may well be an unexpected change from the other novels you study this year.

It's a good book to read aloud. Perhaps some of you might volunteer to take turns with your teacher to read for the rest of the class.

Group work – exploration

Once the people in your class have finished reading, or re-reading the novel, spend time with your group discussing your reactions to the story. These questions may prove interesting to explore:

- Would you like to visit Narnia? Why?

- How would you have behaved if you had been Lucy when she first entered the land?

- Why is this book a fantasy?

Writing your own fantasy

The main assignment for you to attempt after reading C. S. Lewis's book is to try to write your own fantasy about a 'made-up' land. You may work:

- as a group of three or four
- in pairs
- on your own.

If you choose to write on your own, make sure you arrange with either your teacher, a friend, or someone at home to read your work as you go, and offer suggestions.

The fantasy you write is to be written for people of **your own age group**. So you are trying to write a book that **you** and your friends would enjoy reading.

Preparation

Read as many fantasies as you can so that you come to understand this kind of story really well. You might read the other Narnia books by C. S. Lewis and *The Wizard of Oz*, in which humans explore fantasy lands; or books such as J. R. R. Tolkien's *The Hobbit* and Ursula Le Guin's *The Wizard of Earthsea* which are set in entirely new worlds; or fantasies such as Kenneth Grahame's *The Wind in the Willows*, *Watership Down* by Richard Adams or E. H. White's *Charlotte's Web*, in which the main characters are animals.

A suggested approach

Here are some suggestions and guidelines to help you get started. They are written for people who will be working with others, but those of you who want to write on your own will find them useful too.

1. Look carefully through *The Lion, the Witch and the Wardrobe* to see what things a book like this should contain.

- Make a list of what you find, and keep it as a checklist for when your book is ready for publishing.

- There is no map of Narnia in this novel. Include a map of your fantasy land on the checklist, as one of the illustrations.

Decide early about how many illustrations you will include; so that once you've finished the writing you can choose only the best sections for illustration. Use *The Lion, the Witch and the Wardrobe* as a guideline.

2. Think about what sort of land you will create – collect as many ideas from the group as you can, before deciding on anything definite. You need to consider:

⬤ Whether your land will be in the future or the past, or whether it will be timeless.

⬤ What the countryside is like.

⬤ What or who are the inhabitants of the land? Do they have any problems? Are they happy?

⬤ How do outside people get to this land, and how do they leave it?

⬤ What happens to them when they're in the land?

⬤ Who are the outside characters you want? What do they do?

⬤ How do they feel about being in the land?

3. Once you have sorted out as much as you need to be able to start planning your story, work together to write a plan. The plan will need to be in order from beginning to end, and you will need to work out which person in the group will write which parts, so the work can be divided. Your plan will need to be very clear, so that each person knows exactly where to start and where to finish, what has happened 'before' the part he or she is writing, and what will happen after.

Ask your teacher to check your plan to make sure that you haven't forgotten anything.

4. Spend some time talking about your main characters. Describe them and make a 'reference chart' for the characters so that you can refer to it as you write.

5. Do the same thing with a map of your fantasy land. Pin the map on the wall, or in the centre of your desks so that you can all refer to it when necessary.

6. Discuss whether there is anything else you need to do before you start writing. Once you're sure that everybody knows exactly what they are responsible for, you can start on the **hard work** of writing the **first draft**.

● Use every second line of the page for this draft to make revising easier.

● Use your group members to comment as you go, and ask your teacher to help you when you need it.

● Remember, if you have to change any part of the plan let the others know. It could affect what they're doing.

7. After each section of the first draft is completed, arrange it in the order you have planned, and organise regular 'stops' in your writing for the group to read everything done so far, before continuing.

8. When you have finished the whole first draft, go back and read it through together, chapter by chapter. Note any corrections or alterations you wish to make as you read.

● You will need to decide whether you will redraft your own writing, or somebody's else's – but remember, as you do the second draft that the story is now a **whole**, not just a series of chapters any more. Make sure the whole group is satisfied with the ending!

9. When your second draft is finished, you might like to give it to another group to edit, or to your teacher, before you make it ready for 'publication'.

10. Now decide upon illustrations. What will you include? Where will you put the map? What will the cover be like? Is the title a good one? Go back to the checklist you made earlier.

11. As you write the final draft you'll need to make sure that you leave enough room on each page for the binding.

12. Now you can put your story together, and number the pages. You're finished! It's time to relax and enjoy reading your book, and the books that the rest of the people in the class have written.

Reflection

You might enjoy the opportunity to reflect in your journal about writing your own fantasy novel. These questions might help to focus your thinking:

- What did you learn about fantasy?
- Why do you think people write fantasies?
- What did you enjoy most about writing your story?
- What did you learn from writing your own story?
- Has writing your own story helped you to appreciate the work of other writers of fantasy novels?

You might wish to share this writing with your teacher or your group.

Further reading

Richard Adams, *Watership Down*
Joan Aiken, *Whispering Mountain*
Frances Hodgeson Burnett, *The Secret Garden*
Lewis Carroll, *Alice in Wonderland*
Susan Cooper, *Over Sea, Under Stone*
Michael Ende, *The Neverending Story*
Alan Garner, *Elidor, The Weirdstone of Brisingamen*
Kenneth Grahame, *The Wind in the Willows*
Russell Hoban, *The Mouse and his Child*
Ursula Le Guin, *The Wizard of Earthsea*
C.S. Lewis, The Narnia books
Mary Norton, *The Borrowers*
Phillipa Pearce, *Tom's Midnight Garden*
J. R. R. Tolkien, *The Hobbit*
Cynthia Voigt, *Building Blocks*
Diana Wynne Jones, *The Magicians of Caprona*

12 Conflict in the novel

The Boy Who Was Afraid, Armstrong Sperry
Mrs Frisby and the Rats of NIMH, Robert C. O'Brien
The Cay, Theodore Taylor
The Silver Sword, Ian Serraillier

This chapter gives you the opportunity to study one of these four novels. Each of these novels concerns a young person, or group of young people, who are remote from us in both time and place. Their stories tell us much about these remote times and places and show the courage of the characters in overcoming the difficult situations they face.

As well as looking at the courage of the characters in these novels, this chapter focuses on **conflict**. After studying one of the novels, you should understand the different kinds of conflict and why conflict is vital to all novels. You should then be able to think more carefully about using the different kinds of conflict in your own writing.

To the teacher

This chapter has been designed so that you can either use one of these four novels for the whole class, or use more than one novel and allow different groups to choose what they read and study.

The Boy Who Was Afraid

Before reading the novel – prediction

Read the opening three paragraphs of the novel. By yourself, write a list of the problems and adventures that you feel Mafutu will encounter.

When you have finished, compare your predictions with others in your group. Discuss your writing and make a group list.

Keep your list and the group list until after you have finished the novel. Then see how well you were able to predict what would happen.

After reading the novel – exploration

Group discussion

Talk in your group about the novel in order to clarify your thoughts on it. You may wish to consider the following questions:

1. Which part or parts did you find most exciting?

2. Did you find any incidents hard to believe?

3. Did reading the novel make you want to visit the Polynesian Islands?

4. How do you feel about

● the Polynesian way of life?

● the way in which the islanders coped with their environment?

Journal writing

You may enjoy spending ten minutes or so writing in your journal about how you would feel if you'd been caught up in either Mafatu's dilemma – of being afraid of the sea – or in some of his adventures.

On the other hand, you may wish to write about something which you are afraid of, or a fear which you have conquered.

Mrs Frisby and the Rats of NIMH

Before reading the novel – prediction

Read the publisher's blurb on the first page and the note 'About the Author' at the end of the book.

When you have finished, compare your predictions with those of other students in your group. Discuss what you have written and make a group list.

Working by yourself, write a list of Mrs Frisby's problems and adventures with the rats that you feel she will encounter as she seeks their help and learns of their past.

Keep your list and your group list until after you have finished the novel. Then see how well you were able to predict what would happen.

After reading the novel – exploration

Group discussion

Talk in your group about the novel in order to clarify your thoughts on it. You may wish to consider the following questions:

1. Which incident did you find most exciting?

2. Did you find any of the incidents hard to believe?

3. What sort of life do the rats plan for themselves?

4. Why do the humans feel they must kill these particular rats?

5. Which incidents do you think best show how Mrs Frisby is brave or resourceful?

6. Did the novel help you to appreciate the life styles and difficulties of small animals?

7. The novel is based on the fact that live animals are used for experiments. Do you think it is right for this to happen?

The Cay

Before reading the novel – prediction

Read the publisher's blurbs on the back cover and the first page (of the Puffin edition).

Working by yourself, write a list of the problems and adventures that you think Phillip will face.

When you have finished, compare your predictions with other students in your group. Discuss what you have written and and make a group list.

Keep your lists until after you have finished the novel. Then check to see how well you were able to predict what would happen.

After reading the novel – exploration

Group discussion

Talk in your group about the novel in order to clarify your thoughts on it. You may wish to consider the following questions:

1. What impact did the novel make on you?

2. Theodore Taylor makes it clear in his dedication that he wants the very young to 'know and understand'. Does this seem to be his purpose in writing the book?

3. What relevance does the book have for you?

4. What was responsible for Phillip's prejudice against Negroes?

5. How does Phillip lose his prejudice?

6. What incident in the novel did you find most exciting?

7. Theodore Taylor describes many of the survival techniques that Timothy used. Which of these did you find most interesting? Which do you think was most useful to Phillip?

8. Select some occasions on which Phillip showed courage. What do you think enabled him to act bravely on each of these occasions?

Journal writing

Here are some topics that you might enjoy writing about in your journal:

● Any prejudices you have.

● How you think you would cope with being blind.

● How you think you would have acted if you had been Phillip.

The Silver Sword

Before reading the novel – prediction

Read the publisher's blurbs on the back cover and the first page. Look at the titles of each chapter and flick through the book looking at the illustrations.

Working by yourself, write a list of the difficulties and adventures that you think the four young people will experience on their journey from Poland to Switzerland.

When you have finished, compare your predictions with those of other students in your group. Discuss what you have written and make a group list.

Keep your list and your group list until after you have finished the novel. Then see how well you were able to predict what would happen.

After reading the novel – exploration

Group discussion

Talk in your group about the novel in order to clarify your thoughts on it. You may wish to consider the following questions:

1. What impact did the novel have on you?

2. Which incident did you find most exciting?

3. Which part of the book did you find the most moving?

4. Did you find any coincidences hard to believe?

5. Which incident best shows us the courage and resourcefulness of Ruth?

6. Which incident gives us the clearest insight into Jan's character?

7. Why do you think Ian Serraillier chose to tell some of the incidents through the eyes of other people such as the British officer and Captain Greenwood?

Journal writing

One reason we read novels is to increase our experience of the world. Did you find *The Silver Sword* worthwhile from this point of view?

● What did you learn about human nature from reading the book?

● What did you learn about the impact of war on the people of Europe?

● What effect did the war have on (a) Ruth, (b) Edek and (c) Jan?

Conflict

Conflict is the struggle between two opposing forces. When one character struggles against another (for example, Superman fighting against a criminal) that is **external conflict**. Another example of external conflict would be one group of people opposing another. In westerns we see the goodies versus the baddies, the farmers against the ranchers, the cowboys versus the Indians. In crime thrillers the criminals fight the forces of law and order.

Internal conflict occurs when characters struggle with themselves or their consciences. For example, a girl might have to think hard to decide whether to hand in a purse she found in the street or to keep it and the money inside. A conflict that many teenagers face is whether to stay at school and complete their education or to leave early and try to start earning money as soon as possible.

Another kind of conflict that occurs in many novels is **conflict with the environment**. This occurs when characters have to survive in a hostile environment. Examples of this would be characters trying to survive in a desert, in the Antarctic, on a desert island, in a bushfire or in a snow-storm.

Read the following comic strips and look at the different conflicts in each of them.

the PHANTOM
LADY DIANA WILL HAVE BABY IN SKULL CAVE. IS EXPECTED.
BY WHOM? WHAT DO YOU THINK, GRANDPA MOZZ?
21 PHANTOM GENERATIONS BORN IN THIS PLACE. GREAT TRADITION MUST NOT BE BROKEN.
FALK & BARRY 1/22
BABY MUST BE BORN IN SKULL CAVE.
ASK HIM!
SHH, REX. IT'S NOT OUR BUSINESS.
ASK "HIM" WHAT?
SHALL YOUR FORTHCOMING CHILD BE BORN IN THE SKULL CAVE, AS WERE YOU, AND 20 PHANTOMS BEFORE YOU?
FALK & BARRY 1/23
THAT'S FOR THE MOTHER TO SAY. I HOPE SHE'LL DECIDE AGAINST IT!
WHAT?!
TIMES CHANGE, MOZZ. MODERN CITY WOMEN GO TO HOSPITALS. IT'S SAFER.
SAFER? WHAT CAN SHE FEAR? A GREAT CAT? A PYTHON? AN ENEMY?
YOU DON'T WANT YOUR BABY BORN HERE, O GHOST WHO WALKS?
FALK & BARRY 1/24
SHE NEED HAVE NO FEAR, O GHOST WHO WALKS. THE BANDAR WILL GUARD HER AGAINST ALL DANGER!
THAT'S NOT WHAT I MEAN, GURAN.
GRR.
GRR.
I'D PREFER DIANA HAVING OUR BABY IN A MODERN HOSPITAL... IN CASE OF DIFFICULTIES.
DIFFICULTIES? JUST HAVING A BABY?
OUR WOMEN HAVE BABIES IN THE FIELD... BY A STREAM... ANYWHERE. DIFFICULT? IT'S EASY!
FALK & BARRY 1/25
CHIEF GURAN... YOU HAVE A BABY! THEN TELL US IF IT IS SO EASY!
?!
TOMORROW: DIANA
YOU'RE OKAY, DIANA. NO PROBLEMS. WE'LL RESERVE A HOSPITAL ROOM FOR YOU.
SO SOON, DOCTOR? I'VE TIME.
HOSPITALS ARE SO CROWDED. IT'S NECESSARY TO BOOK FAR AHEAD.
NOT YET. I'M NOT SURE I'LL HAVE THE BABY HERE.
NOT HERE? WHERE?
HAVEN'T DECIDED YET. MAYBE... FAR AWAY...
FALK & BARRY 1/26
I SAW THE DOCTOR TODAY. NO PROBLEMS.
NATURALLY, DIANA. WE'LL ARRANGE FOR A HOSPITAL.
I TOLD THE DOCTOR I MAY NOT HAVE THE BABY HERE.
NO? WHERE THEN?
MAYBE... IN THE SKULL CAVE... MAMA..!
OH.. NO!

Group work

1. Draw up a list of all of the different conflicts that you can find in these comic strips. State whether each of these examples is **external** or **internal conflict** or **conflict with the environment**. Be prepared to share your answers with other students in a full class discussion.

2. Using television shows or popular films that you have seen, draw up three separate lists of examples of External Conflict, Internal Conflict and Conflict with the Environment. Work on these lists in your groups. Be prepared to either add your examples to class lists or share them with others in a full class discussion.

Conflict in the novel

1. In your **original groups**, make up a list of all the examples of conflict which you can find in the novel you are studying. Say whether each example involves external or internal conflict or conflict with the environment. Be prepared to justify your decisions to other students.

2. Form **new groups** with two members of your group staying where they are and two members joining another group. Ask your teacher to help you to form these new groups.

3. In your new groups, compare your list with that from the other group. Discuss anything you disagree about. Check with your teacher if necessary.

4. In your new groups, choose examples of two different kinds of conflict in the novel.

   Show how the examples of conflict you have chosen:

   ● play a part in helping Mafatu overcome his fear of the sea, **or**

   ● help Phillip to overcome his prejudice towards Negroes or enable him to survive on the Cay, **or**

   ● help build up the young people's determination to succeed and bring them closer to their journey's end – Switzerland.

5. Show how conflict helps build up **suspense**. Take notes as you discuss these problems so that you can explain your solutions to your original groups and your teacher.

6. Return to your **original groups** and report on your discussion. As a result you should have a sound understanding of what conflict is, the various kinds of conflict that occur in *The Boy Who Was Afraid, Mrs Frisby and the Rats of NIMH, The Cay* or *The Silver Sword* and they way in which conflict builds up suspense and helps the plot to develop.

7. As a group, take one other novel or short story you all know and discuss the conflicts the central character is faced with. Write some notes for your teacher to show that you understand what you have been discussing.

Optional activities

1. As a group make a **poster** or a **collage**, for your classroom notice board, which illustrates the theme of the novel, **or** as a group, design a cover for the novel to be displayed on the notice board. Firstly check with the librarian and look at a number of book covers so that you can be sure of what needs to be included.

2. What is **courage**?
In Harper Lee's novel, *To Kill a Mockingbird*, Atticus Finch says to his son Jem:
   'I wanted you to see what real courage is, instead of getting the idea that courage is a man with a gun in his hand. It's when you know you're licked before you begin but you begin anyway and you see it through no matter what. You rarely win, but sometimes you do.'

   In your groups:

● Talk about examples of courage that you know about, either through your personal experience or your reading, which fit in with this definition of courage. Ask your teacher if you can share one example from your group with the whole class.

● See if you can come up with a definition of courage that would fit Mafatu, Mrs Frisby, Timothy or Phillip or Ruth, Edek or Jan.

Compare your definition with that of one other group.

3. Write or tell a story that shows what you think courage is. Choose a person whose courage you have admired. It could be someone you:

● know

● have read about in the newspaper or seen on television

● have read a novel about, or

● whose biography you have read.

Telling a story:

● Make some notes about the person you choose. Try to focus on one major conflict that they faced which shows their courage.

● When you have worked out your talk, practice it with the other members of your group.

● When all the members of your group are confident that you can tell your story well, without relying on your notes too much, join together with one other group and swap stories.

● Either choose (or ask your teacher to choose) two students from your group of eight to tell their stories to the whole class.

Writing your story:

● Decide who will be the audience for your story. Apart from your teacher and your group, you might wish to share it with the other group you worked with in this chapter.

● Make some notes on the person you've chosen to write about.

● Select one major incident which shows your person's courage.

● Consider the conflicts that they faced.

● Think about how you can create suspense by describing the conflict or conflicts.

● Write the first draft of your story.

● Look at your first draft and see if you can revise it in any way that will make your story clearer to the audience.

● Ask your friends to proof-read your story to see if they can suggest improvements or help with spelling, punctuation and grammar. If possible, ask your teacher to help too.

● Write your final draft and pass it on to the people who will read your story.

Reflection

You may enjoy the opportunity to put your thoughts and feelings about the novel and the work you have done in this chapter into your journal. Talking about the following points in your groups may help you to be clear about what you have learned as a result of studying *The Boy Who Was Afraid*, *Mrs Frisby and the Rats of NIMH*, *The Cay* or *The Silver Sword*.

Explain what you have learned about:

● courage,

● the idea of conflict in novels.

13 Gumble's Yard

Gumble's Yard by John Rowe Townsend is an exciting story which tells of a series of unusual events that happen to ordinary young people living ordinary lives.

The activities in this chapter are designed to help you to explore this novel so that you will come to understand the characters and the problems they face. They should also help you to learn more about the craft of writing and this should help you when you write your own stories.

Individual and group work – exploration

Spend some time talking in your group about the novel in any way you like, to try and understand it more clearly. You may like to discuss some of the following questions:

1. What did you find most interesting in this novel?

2. What parts of the novel made most impact on you?

3. Which characters seemed most real to you?

4. What did you learn about the life-style of the young people involved in the novel?

Journal writing

The first crisis which Kevin, Sandra, Harold and Jean have to face comes when Walter and Doris desert them, and the four youngsters have to fend for themselves.

Think about how you would feel if you were placed in a similar situation. Write a journal entry describing your feelings and explaining how you think you would cope.

Oral story

Kevin mentions the feud between the boys of St Jude's and the Jungle Army, on page 22. No doubt his gang from the Jungle had many adventures.

Do you remember any adventures you had in a gang when you were younger? Discuss your adventures in your small group and decide on one you'd like to tell. If you have any problems thinking of an adventure with a gang, try telling about any exciting incident that happened to you. On the other hand, you might like to tell a story about any incident from your childhood that you are reminded about by an incident in *Gumble's Yard*.

● Practise your story in your own group.

● Move to a new group made up of four people, each from different groups, to tell your story.

● After each student has told their story, choose one from each group to tell the whole class.

The novel as literature

Work on each of the following, making notes for a whole class discussion.

1. The beginning and the ending are particularly important parts of any novel.

   The beginning
   In the first two chapters, Townsend introduces the characters and their environment and outlines the problem they face.

   The ending
   In the last chapter the author ties up the complicated situation and clears up all the unexplained action. The problems that the characters faced are solved.

   Look closely at how John Rowe Townsend writes the beginning and the ending of *Gumble's Yard*. Two of you could prepare notes on Chapters 1 and 2 and the other two on Chapter 14.

2. **Suspense**
   If you have worked through the chapter, 'Creating Suspense', you may find it interesting and worthwhile to examine Townsend's use of suspense in this novel. Three different ways in which a writer can arouse suspense are:

● to leave us uncertain about what will happen,

● to hint about future events,

● to arouse our curiosity and not satisfy it.

Make notes of examples of suspense from the novel under each of these headings. One pair in your group could look at Chapters 1–6 and the other pair Chapters 7–12. Be prepared to explain to the rest of the class the examples of suspense which you feel are most successful.

3. **Who tells the story?**
   Kevin is both the main character and the narrator.

   What are the advantages of the main character telling the story?

   In what ways would it have been a different story if it had been told by Sandra, Dick, Harold, Jean or Tony? Discuss how each of these would have given a different view of the story?

4. **Other features of the novel**
   Make some notes on the following features of Townsend's writing in *Gumble's Yard*:

   his description of the physical environment – especially of the Jungle, of Walter's house and of Gumble's yard.

   the detail that Townsend gives us about the Thompson family, their relationships with one another and the kind of life they lead. Give some examples of the details that are given.

   the way the closing scene balances the opening scene. Why does Townsend provide this balance?

   the way the author blends the extraordinary (fighting gangsters) with the ordinary (the newspaper round, the classroom and cleaning the house).

Whole class discussion

Your teacher will organise a class discussion so that you can share your ideas on these four aspects of Townsend's writing in *Gumble's Yard*. Make sure you are thoroughly prepared for the discussion.

You might decide to take one of the four topics each so that you share your group's contribution to the discussion. However you should make sure that each of you takes notes on each topic.

Group work – drama
Crime stories

1. Bring five objects to school which could be clues to a crime.

2. Taking on the role of detective, show your clues to your group and explain to them how the clues helped you solve the crime.

3. Choose the best of your group's detective stories and have that group member explain his crime story to the whole class.

4. As a group, choose the best five objects which will serve as clues for a group drama presentation.

5. Once you have selected the five clues, work out your story and how you will present it as a piece of drama.

6. Rehearse your drama and present it to the whole class.

Individual work – writing your own story

On page 57, Kevin says: 'Telling a story always gives me confidence. It makes me feel I'm in control of events, and can make things come right.'

Write a story to be read by the others in your group, your teacher, or another group either in your class or in another class at your school.

Consider Kevin's comment and, if you wish, use the opportunity to write about events that are important to you that you'd like to be able to control.

A suggested approach

1. Firstly work out your story-line and write a plan of the events in your story.

2. Consider using some of the techniques you've learnt about from reading and studying *Gumble's Yard*:

- having the main character telling the story;

- describing the physical environment if it is important to your story;

- setting your story in an environment you know well;

- using some of the techniques of suspense you've become aware of;

- making sure your introduction introduces the characters and the environment in which they live and outlines the problems they face;

- making sure the ending clears up anything that hasn't been explained, as well as solving all the problems which your characters have faced;

3. Perhaps you could include:

- a map

- some illustrations

4. After you have written a first draft of your story go through it carefully. Make sure that the meaning you want the reader to get from your story is quite clear. See if you can find any ways to improve your writing. Check on your spelling, punctuation and grammar.

    Ask some of your friends to check your story in much the same way. If possible, show it to your teacher asking him or her if you have mastered the technique you've tried.

5. Produce your final draft for your pre-determined audience to read.

Further reading

John Rowe Townsend, *Good-bye to Gumble's Yard*
This sequel to *Gumble's Yard* is set two years later and concerns the Thompson family and their move from the Jungle to the new housing estate of Westwood.

John Rowe Townsend, *Pirate's Island*
Although this novel was written later, it precedes *Gumble's Yard* in time. It is set in the Jungle in 1946 and features some of the same characters including Sheila Woodrow (aged twelve) who becomes Kevin's English teacher.

John Rowe Townsend, *Hell's Edge*
C. D. Lewis, *The Otterbury Incident*
E. Kästner, *Emil and the Detectives*
L. H. Evers, *The Racketty Street Gang*

14 Sounder

Sounder, by W. H. Armstrong, is a very moving story which shows the poverty and harsh conditions experienced by the Negro people living in the South of the United States of America. It highlights their degrading treatment by the whites and their courage, endurance and determination to survive.

The activities in this chapter are designed to give you an opportunity to look at why W. H. Armstrong wrote *Sounder* and to respond to what happens in the novel.

One of the activities asks you to look closely at the characters in the novel. Other activities ask you to explore the world of the book or to relate the book to your own world.

Group work – exploration

After you have all read *Sounder*, talk with the other people in your group about the book. Make notes for yourself as your group talks, to help you make sure you understand as much as possible.

Do you have any questions about the book? Ask your group, and work them out together. If you have any problems, ask your teacher for help.

1. Some questions that may help you if you're not sure where to start include:

- What feelings did the book arouse in you?
- How did you feel about the family's standard of living?
- Can you understand why the father stole the ham?
- Do you think he was justified in stealing it?
- Why did the mother return the ham?
- How did you feel when the boy took the cake to his father in gaol?
- What kind of person do you think the mother was?
- Why did the boy desperately want to learn to read?

● Why did the author draw parallels between Sounder and his master at the end of the novel?

2. Choose three or four incidents during the novel and discuss the following points in relation to each incident.

● How would you have felt if you had been the boy?

● How do you think you would have behaved if you had been the boy?

3. Did you notice the way the boy supressed his anger by using his imagination? One incident in which he does this starts on page 55. Is this a technique you could use?

Studying the novel: 1. Plot and themes

Individual work

When all the people in your group are sure that they understand the novel, think about the following questions on your own, and jot down some notes about them.

1. William H. Armstrong shows us the very close relationship between Sounder and his master throughout the novel. Find examples to show how he does this.

2. Judging from the Author's Note, among other things, the novel is not just about the dog Sounder. What do you think it is about? Why do you think William H. Armstrong used the title *Sounder*?

3. What is the author trying to tell us, or teach us in this story?

4. What do you think are the main events of the novel?

Group work

1. Read out to your group what you thought about each question, and then discuss each question in order.

2. Allocate each member of your group one question to be in charge of, and share all your ideas on each question so that the person can take down notes that contain the whole group's ideas on his or her question.

The events of the story, and the way in which they are arranged, make up the **plot** of the novel; and the ideas which the writer wants to make clear by telling the story are the **theme** or themes of the novel. The four questions you have looked at in your groups were all to do with **theme** and **plot** in this novel.

3. Check back over your work on the four questions. What do you feel are the main themes in *Sounder*? Check your ideas with your teacher.

● Choose **one** of the themes you have selected, and make up a chart for display on the class notice board. List as many books, films, short stories, songs, and television shows that you can think of that have the same theme as the one you selected.

● When your group has done all it can, ask the teacher-librarian and your teacher if they can help you add more to your list. You might use these lists, or ones made up by other groups in the class, when you're looking for something to read. And you can add to your list as you come across new titles.

2. Character

The Character Game

In your group, make up a list of adjectives that describe the following characters from *Sounder*. Try to come up with about ten for each.

● the boy

● the father

● the mother

● the sheriff

Here are a few suggestions to get you started:

poor	hard-working	dishonest
forgiving	concerned	powerful
powerless	ashamed	careful
rude	angry	hungry

Write each adjective on a separate card, so that your group has made 40 cards, each containing a different word that describes one of the four characters. On a large piece of card or paper, draw up this framework:

THE MOTHER	THE BOY
THE SHERIFF	THE FATHER

Swap the adjective cards that you made up with another group, so that you are not using cards that you made yourselves, and then deal out the cards to your group, so that you have 10 cards each.

RULES

- The aim of this game is to be the first player to get rid of all 10 cards, by placing them, in turn, on the character they **best** describe.

- As your turn comes, place **one** of your adjective cards on the space you decide – and explain to the other players your reasons for putting it there.

- Other players may **challenge** if they do not agree with your placement.

- **All** players must agree to accept the adjective in the place where it is put before you can leave the card there.

- If you are challenged and cannot provide good evidence of why your choice is correct, you must keep the card and the next player has a turn.

- You cannot shift a card once it has been challenged (until your next turn). You must either:
  (a) convince players that you are right (you can use the book for evidence)
  (b) take your card back

- The person to the left of the dealer begins.

N.B. This game can be played again with different adjective cards if you want, or with different characters.

Additional activities

Most of the following activities have been designed for groups of four. As a group, choose two activities to work on. If you wish to work in a different sized group or by yourself, check with your teacher before beginning your activities.

1. Write the script of an interview session in which the author of *Sounder*, W. H. Armstrong, is questioning any three of these characters to gain information for his novel:
   - the boy
   - the father
   - the mother
   - the sheriff
   - the white-haired old man
   - the store-keeper who buys the walnut kernels from the mother
   - one of the people from the big house down the road
   - the red-faced man from the gaol.

   You can go on to tape the interview with these characters if you wish, and then play your tape, or act out your interview for the rest of the class. Ask them to comment on your work so that you will know how well you have prepared the interview.

2. Compile a group anthology of poetry which you might write in response to this book. You might arrange the poems into **themes** similar to those you found in the novel.

3. Survey three people outside school for their comments on the statement: **All men are equal under the law**. Take notes on their responses (a tape-recorder might be helpful) and then write up a summary of what they said. Present your survey to the class or to your teacher, including your own comments and opinions on what the people said, and any news items or articles that helped you form your own opinion.

4. The boy's mother often told him stories 'from the chapel'. Look up the Bible and find the original story of either (a) Joseph, (b) David and Goliath, or (c) Shadrach, Meshach and Abednego. Read the story, work out how you can present it as a play, rehearse it, and perform your drama for the whole class. Check with your teacher before you decide which story to do, so that different groups can choose different stories.

   If you choose the story of Joseph, you might be interested in listening to the record of the musical *Joseph and the Amazing Technicolour Dreamcoat* by Andrew Lloyd Webber and Tim

Rice. Ask your teacher or the librarian if they can help you to find and borrow a copy. As you introduce your play, explain why you think this was the boy's favourite story.

The story of Shadrach is also contained on an album called *Golden Gate Quartet* (CBS 88172). In introducing either the story of Shadrach, or the story of David and Goliath, explain to the class why these may have been popular stories among the Negroes in the Southern states of the U.S.A.

5. Make a collage of pictures, poems and writing that will convey to the class your idea of the major themes in the novel *Sounder*.

6. Discuss this question: Did the father deserve the treatment he received for stealing the ham? Divide your group into two pairs, one of which will act as the **prosecution** and the other as the **defence**.

   The **prosecution** will prepare a case **against** the boy's father.

   The **defence** will prepare a case **for** the father.

   Prepare your cases for an outside judge, such as the Principal, or Deputy, another teacher, another class, a volunteer parent – somebody who is not as familiar with the story of *Sounder* as you. When both sides of the question have been heard, ask the judge to 'pass sentence' telling you which of the two arguments was the more convincing.

7. Write your own short story for people in your class to read. *Sounder* is unusual in that we do not know the names of any of the characters in the story, apart from Sounder himself, even though we get to know the characters fairly well. You could try to idea that you want to convey, and then shaping your plot and characters to suit. Ask your group to act as editors for you, then give your final draft to one other group for a written comment before you present your story to the whole class.

8. The song 'Lonesome Valley' recurs throughout the novel like a theme song in a film which is used to highlight important moments. Throughout *Sounder*, this song is associated with the boy's mother. If you do not know the song, ask your teacher to play a recording of it for you, and then discuss why the song is used with the mother in this way.

15 Bridge to Terabithia

Katherine Paterson

Bridge to Terabithia, by Katherine Paterson, is a sensitive novel which looks at the friendship between Jesse Aarons and Leslie Burke. It explores the joys and difficulties they faced in growing up.

Leslie and Jesse create the magic kingdom of Terabithia as a place where they can be free from the troubles of the world. The strength that Jesse gains from his relationship with Leslie and from the world of Terabithia makes it possible for him to survive the most dreadful event of his life.

By exploring the world of this novel, you should come to understand Jesse and Leslie and the problems they meet. By looking at their lives you may be better equipped to confront similar difficulties in your own life.

This chapter also contains a drama activity for the whole class. Like Terabithia, drama offers more than an escape from reality. It can help you by developing your imagination and by giving you greater confidence to deal with new situations.

Group discussion – exploration

When you have finished reading the novel, it is important to spend some time talking about it with other members of your group and, if possible, your teacher. This should help you to understand the novel more clearly. It should also enable you to understand the characters, their thoughts and their actions.

Talk about the novel in any way you like. Discuss the things that interested you most. Ask questions about anything that puzzled you.

The following points may also be worth discussing in your exploration of the novel:

1. Discuss Jesse's relationship with the other members of the family:
   ● May Belle
   ● Brenda and Ellie
   ● Joyce Ann

- his mother
- his father

One way of doing this might be to:

- look at the incidents in the novel that involve Jesse and each member of his family
- use these incidents to show what Jesse thinks of each person and what each person thinks of Jesse

2. Consider Leslie's relationship with her parents.

3. Look closely at the growth of the relationship between Jesse and Leslie. One of the setbacks in their relationship comes when Leslie helps her father repair their house (Chapter 7, 'The Golden Room'). What does Jesse learn from this experience?

Development of character

One of Katherine Paterson's concerns in this book is about how and why people change.

- A major change in Leslie comes with the incident when she helps Janice Avery (in Chapter 7 'The Golden Room'). In what way does Leslie change as a person? What is responsible for this change in Leslie? Look at page 84 for clues to these questions.

If you are particularly interested in the craft of writing you should look at:

- The conflict between Jesse and Janice leading to the letter trick in Chapter 5, 'The Giant Killers'. Think about why this conflict is important to the later scene.

- Katherine Paterson's Newbery Award speech at the end of this chapter. In it she explains how she included these scenes in the second draft of the novel. Her editor had suggested that we need to see Leslie grow and change. Katherine Paterson used the memory of her school days to create the character of Janice Avery.

- One way to see the changes in Jesse is to look at him at the beginning and at the end of the novel. Consider the difference between the person who wants to be the fastest kid in the fifth grade and Jesse when he *becomes* the fastest kid in the fifth grade.

● Another way to see how Jesse has changed is to look carefully at the final chapter. Think about what Jesse has learned. In particular look at what he thinks during and after his conversation with Mrs Myers.

Building the bridge

Building the bridge to Terabithia also shows how much Jesse has changed. It is important to understand why Jesse builds the bridge.

● Look back at the beginning of Chapter 7, 'The Golden Room', and see how Jesse felt going to Terabithia without Leslie. Also look at how he felt about May Belle and Joyce Ann as companions at that time. His comment at the end of that chapter, 'How could he trust everything that mattered to him to a sassy six-year-old?' is also interesting.

● Read the final chapter 'Building the Bridge'. Consider especially Jesse's thought, 'It was up to him to pay back to the world in beauty and caring what Leslie had loaned him in vision and strength.'

● Look at the second last paragraph of Katherine Paterson's speech. Here she explains why Jesse built the bridge.

● The final chapter is not just about building the bridge to Terabithia. It is also about Jesse building a bridge from the horror of Leslie's death to hope for the future.

● Look carefully at the role Mrs Myers plays in building that bridge between despair at Leslie's death and hope for the future.

Leslie's death

Most of us find it very difficult to accept the death of members of our family or people close to us. We also find the thought of our own death rather difficult to come to terms with. Most readers, therefore, find Leslie's death difficult to believe or to accept.

'Of course, the child can't die by lightning. No editor would ever believe that.' This comment appears in Katherine Paterson's speech and it shows how difficult we find it to accept a death like Leslie's. *Bridge to Terabithia* allows us to experience at second hand the death of Leslie, and Jesse's attempts to come to terms with it.

One reason we read books is to increase our experience of life. Looking at the problems that the characters face often helps us to face some of the problems and harsh realities of our own lives. Katherine Paterson's speech shows us clearly how, in writing the book, she came to terms with the death of those close to her and with her own death. Reading the novel may help us in a similar way.

The Newbery Medal speech tells us a great deal about how Katherine Paterson wrote *Bridge to Terabithia*.

● You may be able to learn some things that will be useful for your own writing by discussing the speech.

● The author gives us hints about the forthcoming disaster in the last paragraphs of Chapter 7 (p. 90), Chapter 8 (p. 99) and Chapter 9 (p. 107). Examine these paragraphs and discuss how they prepare us for Leslie's death. You may be able to use this technique in your own writing.

● Katherine Paterson has chosen the title of each chapter carefully. Chapter 10, 'The Perfect Day', has an **ironic** title. That is, it says one thing, yet means exactly the opposite. Discuss how in one sense the title is true and in another sense the opposite is true.

● On page 115 Jesse says 'This one perfect day of his life was worth anything he had to pay.' This statement is also ironic. When he made the statement Jesse thought it was true. If he had thought back later he would certainly not have thought it to be true.

On reading back over that paragraph how do you feel about Jesse saying that, when you know the price he has to pay? You may be able to use this technique in your own writing.

The magic kingdom

> I know . . . it could be a magic country like
> Narnia, and the only way you can get in is by
> swinging across on this enchanted rope.
>
> *Bridge to Terabithia* (page 49)

If you have read *The Lion, The Witch and the Wardrobe* by
C. S. Lewis, you will know what Leslie is talking about here.

To get to Narnia one has to go through the magic wardrobe:
To get to Terabithia one has to swing on the enchanted rope.

At first Jesse sees Terabithia as a 'stronghold where everything
seemed possible'. Between the two of them they owned the
world and no enemy, Gary Fulcher, Wanda Kay Moore, Janice
Avery, Jesse's own fears and insufficiencies, nor any of the
foes whom Leslie imagined attacking Terabithia, could ever
really defeat them.

After he comes to accept Leslie's death, Jesse realises 'that
perhaps Terabithia was like a castle where you came to be
knighted. After you stayed for a while and grew strong you
had to move on.'

Whole class work – role play

As a whole class you could try the challenge of creating a
magic kingdom in your classroom, or the drama room; and
improvising a day in the life of the kingdom. Your teacher will
act as director, and will tell you how much time you have for
preparation, and for the role play.

```
*KING          *COURT JESTER      *MINSTRELS      *LADIES IN
*QUEEN         *COURT PHYSICIAN   *BUTLER          WAITING
*PRINCES       *COURT CRIER       *KNIGHTS        *MAIDS
*PRINCESSES    *HIGH PRIEST       *GUARDS         *COOKS
*MAGICIAN      *SEA CAPTAIN       *AMBASSADORS    *VISITORS
```

1. In your groups, begin by making suggestions as to the type of kingdom you would like, and the sorts of people who might live there. Here are some suggestions – but you can use your imagination, as well as any ideas from books you've read, from movies or television:

2. Share your group's list with the lists from other groups in the class, so that you have all your ideas on the blackboard, or on a wall-chart.

   You can now decide what the kingdom will look like. In order to build up a complete picture of the kingdom, each group could take responsibility for describing one aspect of it. One group could make a map of the whole kingdom, indicating the major landforms, towns and borders; other groups could draw, make maps of (or even build!) smaller parts of the kingdom, such as:

   - the palace
   - the villages
   - the forest
   - the central hall of court

   Because there is a lot of work involved with this task of 'Setting the Scene', two groups might combine on a project and work together.

3. Once you have got the setting of your class drama clear, each person will have to decide on the role that he or she will play. Your teacher will help to organise this with you . . .

. . . and when you've decided which role you will play, spend some time on your own, 'getting to know' your character really well. You need to prepare yourself thoroughly for a role play, and one helpful way is to make up a **role card** for yourself. Here is an example:

```
┌─────────────────────────────────────────────┐
│        THE GOVERNESS  .Lucy...                │
│  *Name: Lucinda                               │
│  *born in small country village; orphaned     │
│   at 12; educated in a convent till 18,       │
│   then sent to teach the Royal children.      │
│  *now 28 years old, very religious            │
│  *has refused offer of marriage from the      │
│   Court Secretary                             │
│  *speaks with the Queen each morning to       │
│   report on the children's lessons            │
│  *reads to Queen and Ladies in Waiting in     │
│   the afternoons while they relax after       │
│   luncheon                                    │
│  *NEVER speaks to adult members of Royal      │
│   Family unless spoken to first               │
│  *is often ill, and is always asking the      │
│   Court Physician for something to cure       │
│   her,      etc.                              │
└─────────────────────────────────────────────┘
```

Your role card will help you know exactly what sort of character you are going to play.

4. When you're happy that you have made yourself a life-like character, spend time with the people in your group, to work out how your characters will speak in the magic kingdom. The language that Leslie and Jesse use in Terabithia will give you some clues, but you can once again draw upon your knowledge of the language used by characters in other books, plays, films and TV shows.

5. As a whole class, with your teacher to help you, you will need to focus the scene for your role play. What sort of day will it be in your kingdom?

- a feast day?

- a wedding day?

- a day before a battle?

- a day when the kingdom is under siege?

- the day the old king dies? etc.

6. Once you've set the focus on the particular day, and when all role cards are complete, each person should introduce his or her character to the class, so that you **all** know who you are.

7. When you're all ready . . . enjoy yourselves. Remember that you **are** your character during the role play, and that you must act, speak (and even think!) as your character would in the magic kingdom.

8. When your role play is over, spend some time talking about what happened with your group. Your teacher might share his or her impressions of the drama with you, or you might discuss what it was like to play act without an 'audience', when everyone is involved.

   You might consider that what you've done could be the start of something big! If you would like to work on your role play, and develop it so that you can present it to an audience as a piece of real theatre, it could mean a lot of work. But it could be fun too.

Reflection

Use your journal for reflection on the class role play:

How did you feel while you were (a) preparing your role?
                                                   (b) playing your role?

Do you think that the role play helped you to understand more about the novel *Bridge to Terabithia*? How do you think Jesse felt about playing the role of King of Terabithia?

Have a think about the novel again, and about the parts of the story that you found most interesting, or moving, or puzzling. How do you think you would have behaved if you had been Jesse? You might like to write down your thoughts in your journal, or in some other form, like a poem or a letter, for somebody in your group.

Further reading

If you would like to read some other novels by Katherine Paterson, your library may have some of these:

The writer's reflections

Here is part of a speech given by Katherine Paterson in 1978, after she received the Newbery Medal for 'the most distinguished contribution to American literature for children' for *Bridge to Terabithia*. She talks about the book, and about writing the book . . .

Yet of all the people I have ever written about, perhaps Jesse Aarons is more nearly me than any other, and in writing this book, I have thrown my body across the chasm that had most terrified me.

I have been afraid of death since I was a child – lying stiffly in the dark, my arms glued to my sides, afraid that sleep would seduce me into a land of no awakening or of wakening into judgment.

As I grew up, the fear went underground but never really went away. Then I was forty-one years old with a husband and four children whom I loved very much, my first novel published, a second soon to be and a third bubbling along, friends I cared about in a town I delighted to live in, when it was discovered that I had cancer. I could not in any justice cry 'Why me?' – for no one had been given more of the true wealth of this world than I. Surely as a card-carrying member of the human race some dues must be paid.

But even though the operation was pronounced successful and the prognosis hopeful, it was a hard season for me and my family, and just when it seemed that we were all on our feet again and beginning to get on with life, our David's closest friend was struck and killed by lightning.

If the spring and summer had been hard, they were nothing compared to the fall. David went through all the classical stages of grief, inventing a few the experts have yet to catalogue. In one of these he decided that since Lisa had been good, God had not killed her for her sins but as a punishment for him, David. Moreover,

God would continue to punish him by killing off everyone he loved. I was second on the list, right after his sister Mary.

We listened to him and cried with him, but we could not give Lisa back to him, these mere mortals that he now knew his parents to be.

In January I went to a meeting of the Children's Book Guild of Washington at which Ann Durell of Dutton was to speak. By some chance or design, depending on your theology, I was put at the head table. In the polite amenities before lunch someone said to me: 'How are the children?' – for which the answer, as we all know, is 'Fine.' But I botched it. Before I could stop myself I began really to tell how the children were, leading my startled tablemates deep into the story of David's grief.

No one interrupted me. But when I finally shut up, Ann Durell said very gently, 'I know this sounds just like an editor, but you should write that story. Of course,' she added, 'the child can't die by lightning. No editor would ever believe that.'

I thought I couldn't write it, that I was too close and too over-whelmed, but I began to try to write. It would be a kind of therapy for me, if not for the children. I started to write in pencil on the free pages of a used spiral notebook so that when it came to nothing I could pretend that I'd never been very serious about it.

After a few false starts, thirty-two smudged pages emerged, which made me feel that perhaps there might be a book after all. In a flush of optimism I moved to the typewriter and pounded out a few dozen more, only to find myself growing colder and colder with every page until I was totally frozen. The time had come for my fictional child to die, and I could not let it happen.

I caught up on my correspondence, I rearranged my bookshelves, I even cleaned the kitchen – anything to keep the inevitable from happening. And then one day a friend asked, as friends will, 'How is the new book coming?' and I blurted out – 'I'm writing a book in which a child dies, and I can't let her die. I guess,' I said, 'I can't face going through Lisa's death again.'

'Katherine,' she said, looking me in the eye, for she is a true friend, 'I don't think it's Lisa's death you can't face. I think it's yours.'

I went straight home to my study and closed the door. If it was my death I could not face, then by God, I would face it. I began in a kind of fever, and in a day I had written the chapter, and within a few weeks I had completed the draft, the cold sweat pouring down my arms.

It was not a finished book, and I knew it, but I went ahead and did what no real writer would ever do: I had it typed up and mailed it off to Virginia before the sweat had a chance to evaporate.

There is no span of time quite so eternal as that between the mailing of a manuscript and the reception of an editor's reply. I knew she hated it; that's why she hadn't written or called. It was weird and raw and no good, and she was trying to think of some kind way to tell me that I was through as a writer.

Finally she called. 'I laughed through the first two thirds and cried through the last,' she said. So it was all right. She understood, as she always has, what I was struggling to do. And although she did not know what was happening in my life, she did not break the bruised reed I had offered her but sought to help me weave it into a story, a real story, with a beginning, a middle, and an end.

'We need to see Leslie grow and change,' she said. And suddenly, from the ancient dust of the playground at Calvin H. Wiley School, there sprang up a small army of seventh-grade Amazons led by the dreadful Pansy Something-or-Other, who had terrorized my life when I was ten and not too hard to terrify.

'You must convince us,' Ann Beneduce added, 'that Jesse has the mind of an artist.' This seemed harder, for I certainly don't have Ann's kind of artistic vision. I started bravely, if pompously, reading the letters of Vincent Van Gogh, and when they didn't help, I went, as I often do, to my children.

'David,' I asked, feeling like a spy, 'why don't you ever draw pictures from nature?'

And my nine-year-old artist nature-lover replied, 'I can't get the poetry of the trees.' It is the only line of dialogue that I have ever consciously taken from the mouth of a living person and put into the mouth of a fictitious one. It doesn't usually work, but that time it seemed to.

I have never been happier in my life than I was those weeks I was revising the book. It was like falling happily, if a little crazily, in love. I could hardly wait to begin work in the morning and would regularly forget about lunch. The valley of the shadow which I had passed through so fearfully in the spring had, in the fall, become a hill of rejoicing.

This time when I sent the manuscript off to Virginia I said: 'I know that love is blind, for I have just mailed you a flawless manuscript.'

In time, of course, my vision was restored. I no longer imagine the book to be without flaws, but I have never ceased to love the people of this book – even the graceless Brenda and the inarticulate Mrs. Aarons. And, oh, May Belle, will you ever make a queen? I still mourn for Leslie, and when children ask me why she had to die, I want to weep, because it is a question for which I have no answer.

It is a strange and wonderful thing to me that other people who do not even know me love Jesse Aarons and Leslie Burke. I have given away my own fear and pain and faltering faith and have been repaid a hundredfold in loving compassion from readers like you. As the prophet Hosea says, the Valley of Trouble has been turned into the Gate of Hope.

Theodore Gill has said, 'The artist is the one who gives form to difficult visions.' This statement comes alive for me when I pore over Peter Spier's *Noah's Ark.* The difficult vision is not the destruction of the world. We've had too much practice imagining that. The difficult vision which Mr. Spier has given form to is that in the midst of the destruction, as well as beyond it, there is life and humour and caring along with a lot of manure shoveling. For me those final few words 'and he planted a vineyard' ring with the same joy as 'he found his supper waiting for him and it was still hot.'

In talking with children who have read *Bridge to Terabithia*, I have met several who do not like the ending. They resent the fact that Jesse would build a bridge into the secret kingdom which he and Leslie had shared. The thought of May Belle following in the footsteps of Leslie is bad enough, but the hint that the thumb-sucking Joyce Ann may come as well is totally abhorrent to these readers. How could I allow Jesse to build a bridge for the unworthy? they ask me. Their sense of what is fitting and right and just is offended. I hear my young critics out and do not try to argue with them, for I know as well as they do that May Belle is not Leslie, nor will she ever be. But perhaps some day they will understand Jesse's bridge as an act of grace which he built, not because of who May Belle was but because of who he himself had become crossing the gully into Terabithia. I allowed him to build the bridge because I dare to believe with the prophet Hosea that the very valley where evil and despair defeat us can become a gate of hope – if there is a bridge.

In closing, I want to explain the Japanese word on the dedication page of *Bridge to Terabithia*. The word is *banzai*, which some of you will remember from old war movies. I am very annoyed when writers throw in Italian and German phrases that I can't understand, but suddenly as I wrote the dedication to this book, *banzai* seemed to be the only word I knew that was appropriate. The two characters which make the word up say, 'all years,' but the word itself combines the meanings of our English word *Hooray* with the ancient salute to royalty, 'Live forever!' It is a cry of triumph and joy, a word full of hope in the midst of the world's contrary evidence. It is the word I wanted to say through *Bridge to Terabithia.* It is a word that I think Leslie Burke would have liked. It is my salute to all of you whose lives are bridges for the young.

Banzai!

Acknowledgements

We gratefully acknowledge the following for their permission to reprint copyright material: The Australian Association for the Teaching of English Inc for 'Aunt Jane' by Jonathan Dawson reprinted from *The Bad Deeds Gang and Other Stories* ed. L.M. Hannan and W.G. Tickell (Australian Association for the Teaching of English, 1971);   William Blackwood & Sons Limited for 'The Highwayman' by Alfred Noyes from *Alfred Noyes: Collected Poems*; André Deutsch Ltd for 'I'm the youngest in our house' from *Wouldn't You Like to Know* by Michael Rosen, André Deutsch 1977, and 'I share my bedroom with my brother' from *Mind Your Own Business* by Michael Rosen, André Deutsch, 1974;   Gavin Ewart for 'Arithmetic' by Gavin Ewart from *The Deceptive Grin of the Gravel Porters*, London Magazine Editions;   Roy Fuller for 'The National Union of Children/The National Association of Parents' by Roy Fuller from *Seen Grandpa Lately*;   Heinemann Educational Books Ltd for the extract from *The Thwarting of Baron Bolligrew* by Robert Bolt; James Kirkup for 'The Lonely Scarecrow' from *Refusal to Conform* (Oxford University Press);   Harold Matson Co. Inc. for 'When the Indians' from *A Child's Garden of Verses for the Revolution* by William Eastlake;   Spike Milligan Productions Ltd for 'My Sister Laura' and the accompanying illustration, from *Silly Verse for Kids* (Penguin);   Adrian Mitchell for 'Dumb Insolence' from *Nothingmas Day* by Adrian Mitchell (Allison and Busby);   Bill Naughton for 'Spit Nolan' from *The Goalkeeper's Revenge*, Thomas Nelson and Sons Ltd, assignees of Harrap Limited;   Penguin Books Ltd for 'Nothing to be Afraid Of' from *Nothing to be Afraid Of* by Jan Mark (Kestrel Books, Harmondsworth 1980), copyright © Jan Mark, 1977, 1980, pp. 9–17, reproduced by permission of Penguin Books Ltd, and 'Who's been at the toothpaste?' by Michael Rosen from *You Tell Me* by Roger McGough and Michael Rosen (Kestrel Books, 1979), copyright © Michael Rosen 1979, p. 62;   AD Peters & Co Ltd for 'The Flying Machine' by Ray Bradbury from *The Golden Apples of the Sun* (Hart-Davis MacGibbon Ltd). Reprinted by permission of AD Peters & Co Ltd;   Deborah Rogers Ltd for 'Street Boy' from *Salford Road* copyright © by Gareth Owen 1976. Used by Permission;   Syndication International (1986) Ltd for 'It's the Letrit' from *Cassandra at His Finest and Funniest* (Daily Mirror/Paul Hamlyn);   United Feature Syndicate, Inc. for Peanuts cartoon;   Westbury Music Limited for the lyrics of 'Where Do The Children Play?' by Cat Stevens, reprinted by kind permission of Westbury Music Ltd; Yaffa Character Licensing for the cartoons 'Rip Kirby' and 'The Phantom' © King Features Syndicate, Inc.